Travel That Can Change Your Life

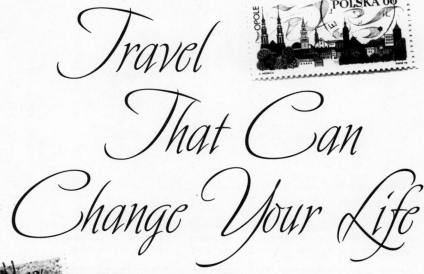

Travel That Can Change Your Life

How to Create a Transformative Experience

Jeffrey A. Kottler, Ph.D.

 Jossey-Bass Publishers
San Francisco

Substantial discounts on bulk quantities of Jossey-Bass books are available to corporations, professional associations, and other organizations. For details and discount information, contact the special sales department at Jossey-Bass Inc., Publishers (415) 433–1740; Fax (800) 605–2665.

For sales outside the United States, please contact your local Simon & Schuster International Office.

Jossey-Bass Web address: http://www.josseybass.com

 Manufactured in the United States of America on Lyons Falls Turin Book. This paper is acid-free and 100 percent totally chlorine-free.

Library of Congress Cataloging-in-Publication Data

Kottler, Jeffrey A.
 Travel that can change your life: how to create a transformative
 experience / Jeffrey A. Kottler. — 1st ed.
   p. cm.—(The Jossey-Bass psychology series)
 Includes bibliographical references and index.
 ISBN 0-7879-0941-6 (alk. paper)
  1. Self-actualization (Psychology) 2. Change (Psychology)
3. Travel—Psychological aspects. I. Title. II. Series.
BF637.S4K68 1997
910'.01'9—dc21
                                97-557

FIRST EDITION
HB Printing 10 9 8 7 6 5 4 3 2 1

Contents

Preface   ix

1 How Travel Has Transformed Itself   1

2 Why People Travel   10

3 Where Are You Going?   30

4 Planning Your Trip   43

5 Doing What Comes Unnaturally   61

6 Refashioning Yourself   77

7 Focusing on People   89

8 If It's Adventure You Are After   103

9 When Things Go Wrong   114

10 Long-Term Versus Brief Travel   132

11 Creating Meaning in Your Travel   148

For Further Reading   167

About the Author   173

Index   175

⤳ *Preface*

There are many good reasons why you might be planning a trip. You may feel the need for a break in your life, a respite from the daily stresses you encounter at work or home. Perhaps you need to get away for a while just to break up the predictable schedules that rule your life. Or you may want to spend time with your family, to escape winter weather, to pursue a romance, to learn something new, to create excitement through adventure, to explore unknown territory, to seek spiritual enlightenment, to solve a personal problem, to act out a fantasy, to attend a wedding or funeral, to conduct business or attend a conference.

It would appear in each of these cases that the traveler's motive is unique. Indeed, if you were to look around the cabin of any airplane you would find a group of people who may all be heading to the same destination for very different reasons. Look deeper, however, and what you will find is that underlying most people's stated reason for the trip is another, often unconscious, desire to change something about themselves and their lives. On some level, each of us uses travel to promote personal transformation. This is true whether you are after a major shift in lifestyle or a minor adjustment in the ways you do business. Regardless of your stated agenda, change of some sort will often result. The only question is whether this change will be intentional, deliberate, and constructive—or accidental, random, perhaps even dangerous.

WHY I WROTE THIS BOOK

I change people for a living. I am a therapist, a teacher and supervisor of other practitioners, an author who writes about the transformations that participants undergo that are part of the therapeutic process. This includes not just students and clients, but teachers and therapists as well.

Throughout much of my professional life, I have often felt like a travel agent. After all, my job has been to help people take holidays away from their daily, often impoverished, lives. I encourage people to visit new places and explore new territory, metaphorically speaking. I help them plan these trips and make appropriate arrangements, and then offer the support that is often needed for those venturing into the unknown.

Like most teachers and therapists, I am both fulfilled and frustrated by my work. I love seeing people change, but the process often happens *so* slowly. Or worse yet—I see people change in my office or classroom but notice that the effects are often transient.

It is sheer arrogance to believe that people in my profession have cornered the market on promoting lasting personal change. Bartenders, hairdressers, taxi drivers, even friends, have been known to help people grow as a result of their interactions. I've wondered if real travel agents don't do the best job of all.

Traveling can bring out in you parts of yourself that can't be accessed any other way. Always looking for more efficient and effective ways to promote personal changes, I realized that most of the constructive growth I've undergone in my own life has not come from books, or the classroom, or even therapy, but from traveling—especially the kind of trip that involves not just the search for new experiences in the world, but also the time and inclination to look within.

WHAT THIS BOOK WILL DO FOR YOU

Everyone knows how to travel. What's the big deal? You see a travel agent, make an airline reservation or hop in the car, and then you're off. You've done your homework. Read a few guidebooks. Talked to friends who have been in the vicinity. Studied a map. Plotted out what you will do and when you will do it.

Of course, you'll have a lovely time. You've worked hard to pay for this trip, or you'll pay off your credit cards after you return. What you're after, mostly, is time away from daily pressures, a chance to relax and see some sights.

If that is indeed what you're after, then this book is definitely not for you. There are already whole bookstores devoted solely to providing the prospective traveler with guides about where to go, what to see and photograph, where to eat and sleep, which places are best avoided, what to buy and where to get the best deals. These books are indispensable. However, their intent is to save you time and inconvenience. The purpose of this book, however, is not so much to inform as to transform you. The goal is to help you explore your motives for traveling and create the type of trip that will most likely accomplish your preferred objectives.

More specifically, you will be encouraged to examine what it is you are looking for and where you might find it, whether in an isolated cabin in the woods, a luxurious resort on a pristine beach, a swirling, congested Third World city, or a dog-sledding expedition in the Arctic. Here are some of the questions we will consider:

- Should you go alone or with members of your family?
- What steps should you take to plan a trip that is most likely to encourage permanent changes in your thinking and behavior?
- How can you structure things in a way to produce unexpected growth and learning?
- What aspects of your travel experience would be most crucial to focus on?
- How can you handle the inevitable things that will go wrong?
- What meaning can you construct from what you experienced?
- How do you follow through on your resolutions and maintain your momentum once you return home?

Travel offers you more opportunities to change your life than almost any other human endeavor. People who structure their journeys in particular ways consistently report dramatic gains in self-esteem, confidence, poise, and self-sufficiency. They enjoy greater intimacy as a result of bonds that were forged under magical and sometimes adverse circumstances. They become more fearless risk takers, better problem solvers, and far more adaptable to ever-changing circumstances. They become more knowledgeable about the world, its fascinating customs, and its diverse people. Finally, travel teaches you most about yourself—about what you miss when you are gone and what you don't, about what you are capable of doing in strange circumstances, about what you really want that you don't yet have.

Regardless of what exactly you are looking for, and where you hope to find it, may travel change your life for the better.

ACKNOWLEDGMENTS

I am grateful to Susan Thompson, Felicia Campbell, Deborah Fraser, Sherrill Wiseman, Carole Taipale, Diane Blau, Cynny Carruthers, and David Holmes for their help in clarifying many of my ideas related to the transformative nature of travel experiences. I especially appreciate the efforts of Pirkko Yukes and Jenny Elliot-Tavano for their assistance in conducting the research related to this project. I also wish to thank my agent, Jean Naggar, and her staff for their encouragement during this journey.

After working together on our fourth project, I am still amazed at how my editor, Alan Rinzler, can help create a coherent book so easily from the stacks of pages I send him.

I am most indebted to Ellen and Cary Kottler, who indulged my wanderlust, made excuses for me as to why I was always in some forsaken place or another, and welcomed me home with open arms.

March 1997

Jeffrey A. Kottler
Las Vegas, Nevada

1

How Travel Has Transformed Itself

We were meant to move. Our ancestors were wanderers, hunters, and gatherers. They followed herds and water. They relocated themselves continuously, depending on the weather and seasons. Our very survival once depended on our mobility. On every continent, tribal communities traveled to where the best opportunities lay—they moved or they died. To this day, we carry this legacy within our genes, programmed over millennia.

Travel has certainly changed over the years, from walking and riding horseback to sitting in bullet trains and supersonic jets. The reasons people travel have evolved considerably as well. Conquest, nomadic wandering, and religious pilgrimage are no longer prime motives for most of us. Still, whether in ancient Babylon or the Australian outback, people used to travel for many of the same purposes we do today: to explore the world, to find better opportunities for work and trade, to seek romance and adventure, always to make a better life.

A BRIEF HISTORY OF RECREATIONAL TRAVEL

Going back a few dozen centuries, the Phoenicians were the first people to travel to any great extent, almost always for business rather than pleasure. Later, sometime around the sixth century B.C., wealthy Greeks were among the first to make journeys purely for entertainment—usually to visit spas, festivals, and of course the Olympic Games. A few centuries later, Romans were the first people to build a tourist industry, complete with an extensive road system, hotels, even a few gladiator shows thrown in for entertainment.

After the decline of the Roman Empire in the first centuries A.D., traveling fell into disrepute except as a means to transport armies to the next battlefield. During the Dark Ages, it simply wasn't safe to be on the road with raiding Mongols and Tartars around; people stayed home. Strangers, visitors, *any* travelers, were viewed with suspicion, and probably with good reason: they may very well have been spies sent to scout out potential pickings or even carriers of bubonic plague.

This attitude was a radical departure from previous eras in which travelers were usually held in high regard. They were a source of news and information, mediators of disputes, messengers of the gods. In the days before the postal system, CNN, faxes, and electronic mail, travelers were the principal means of communication between settlements. This was the case not just with passing along gossip, but also with spreading news of technology. And travelers served other roles as well. From an evolutionary perspective, they were relied upon to diversify the gene pool. The sperm of strangers was needed to bring in new blood.

During the Dark Ages, however, both Christian and Muslim pilgrims began making spiritual journeys to Jerusalem. They braved pirates and robbers, holy wars, famine, and the plague, all to seek renewal of their religious faith. While at first these travelers of varied persuasions tolerated one another in an uneasy truce, eventually things escalated to the point where each group tried to stop the other's freedom of movement. The Christian Crusades were launched at the turn of the twelfth century, a kind of mass travel group mobilized by Pope Urban II and an assortment of other charismatic guides with names like Peter the Hermit and Walter the Penniless.

It is against the backdrop of the Middle Ages that Marco Polo's exploits seem all that more remarkable. Nobody else before or since (with the possible exception of Captain James Cook) has done more to give travel a good name. Over the course of twenty-five years during the middle of the thirteenth century, he crossed the length of China, during which time he served as a soldier, politician, trader, consultant, but most of all, pure traveler in the sense that he loved what strange lands had to teach him. He was never the same again; neither was the entire world after he brought back stories of what he had seen.

What Polo did for land travel, certainly James Cook did for sea journeys five hundred years later. While Prince Henry the Navigator, Christopher Columbus, and Vasco da Gama were also great sailors and explorers, it was Cook who viewed travel as an opportunity for personal growth as well as ambition.

Styles of Travel

In the days of nomads and pilgrims, people traveled light, taking only what they could comfortably carry on their backs. If such journeys precipitated personal enlightenment, it was often because travelers separated themselves from the material world as much as possible. One object of such a quest, after all, was to practice a simpler life.

This style of basic travel was irrevocably altered with the advent of machines for transportation—a mode that, while faster and more comfortable than your own feet, also insulates you from the world you are passing through. Personal change can be far more difficult when you bring your own world with you on the journey. As the technology of travel improved, it became more and more common for even the moderately well-to-do traveler to bring an assortment of possessions that would maintain a degree of comfort and prevent the possibility of intrusive changes in environment. And the comforts of the rich knew no bounds. When the Prince and Princess of Wales visited Egypt in the nineteenth century, they traveled along the Nile aboard a fleet of six ships loaded with supplies. They brought their own chefs and three thousand bottles of champagne. The goal, after all, was to transport part of England with them so they wouldn't be subjected to any disturbing inconveniences.

Early Western Travelers

The nineteenth century was indeed a turning point in the history of recreational travel. Hitherto, the explorers were almost always men, almost always in pursuit of fame, riches, and glory. Their journals are filled with their exploits, with notations of scientific observations, conquered territory, and map coordinates; rarely do we see any mention of personal changes the traveler might have undergone.

Once women began to travel independently, as they did for the first time in any significant numbers in the nineteenth century, the literature on the subject changed dramatically. In an anthology of "maiden voyages," editor Mary Morris concluded that, as with most pursuits, women move through the world differently than men. They face greater risk of harassment, even rape, and this certainly colors their perceptions. More important for our purposes, they write about their experiences more introspectively, with more emotion. Rather than speaking only about what they have charted or conquered, women prefer instead to note their internal reactions to what they have seen.

Morris analyzes women's letters and essays, noting some of the major themes characteristic of their transformative travels. Just as with men, women's journeys are driven by curiosity, by the urge to see what is beyond the horizon. Yet the women travelers of the Victorian era were also fiercely independent, strong-willed, and rebellious. They had to be in order to take what writer Mabel Crawford called the opportunity to improve themselves by means other than crochet-work or embroidery.

Few mavericks did more to advance the cause of women travelers than Ethel Brilliana Tweedie, an English writer who was among the most influential spokespeople for making it socially acceptable to ride a bicycle or horse other than sidesaddle. Once women could ride astride their steeds like men, they could travel much greater distances with considerably less fatigue than before.

Another example of the woman's travel voice is found in the diary of Isabelle Eberhardt, a young woman of the nineteenth century who was far more interested in describing her own internal reactions than the external events she witnessed. Just before her death—from a flash flood in North Africa—she wondered why at home, when she had the comforts of a good diet, warm clothes and shelter, and an oversolicitous mother, the slightest chill would turn into bronchitis. Yet when suffering freezing temperatures on the road, in bare feet and tattered garments, she never even caught a cold. "The human body is nothing, the human soul is all," she concluded.

The Male Contribution

Although the concept of travel as a transformative experience comes primarily from the observations of women travelers of the nineteenth century, men have also contributed to the ways travel turned itself into the potentially growthful experience it is today. Men's observations of the beneficial effects of hardship and crisis led to the development of adventure-based excursions. Programs such as Outward Bound began during the middle of this century as a way to help young men increase their confidence and performance under pressure.

Kurt Hahn, a refugee from war-torn Germany, relocated to Great Britain with a number of radical ideas about how to prepare youth to be more resilient, imaginative, and enterprising. Disabled by sunstroke as a young man, Hahn sought recovery by conquering progressively more difficult physical challenges. He started adventure-oriented travel programs as a way to help people change themselves into more competent and poised beings.

The intent of such programs is to subject participants to a series of difficult challenges in foreign environments that will force them to reach beyond their current levels of competence. This agenda is one of the most potent forces that underscores most any life-changing event, especially when it is combined with some sort of reflective activity to create personal meaning from the experience.

The Democratization of Travel

Until fairly recently in history, travel was limited to the very rich, who traveled for amusement and commerce, or the poor, who relocated themselves to find some place to live and work. The birth of the leisure class made possible opportunities in which people could have the discretionary time, resources, and means to travel for their own amusement, education, and personal growth.

Today, tourism employs more people than any other industry. Incredibly, it is second only to food production in how we spend most of our money. In the United States alone, gift shops sell thirty billion souvenirs a year to people who want reminders of their journeys.

We travel vicariously by watching movies and television, reading books, and listening to stories of action and adventure. We let off steam, here and there, by taking extended weekends when we can. We travel for business occasionally, and that certainly helps—even though most of the time we remain insulated from the place we are visiting. For most people, however, travel has become something to do for a few weeks a year, each precious day of freedom earned through a month's hard labor.

In whatever form recreational travel takes, as a brief interlude or extended sabbatical, it has evolved over time from a necessary annoyance to a cherished holi-day (a holy day in which a sacred event was celebrated). In his historical review of the role excursions have played in our lives, Eric Leed concludes: "Travel has long been a means of changing selves, a method of altering social status, of acquiring fame, fortune, and honor—even a profession for shape changing, for acting has long been an itinerant profession." Travel is thus by its very nature a transformative experience. It also hooks into one of our most basic instincts.

Controlling Territory

We are territorial creatures, not unlike chimpanzees, bears, lions, and other large mammals. The more territory we can cover and control, the more food and resources are available to us. Even though most members of our species have given up the lifestyle of hunters, we can still see remnants of the prestige and power associated with controlling the most space possible. Drive through any city and you can easily detect who is most wealthy and powerful by the size of the home and surrounding property.

We have not only a strong urge to control as much land as possible, but also to see as much territory as we can. Each of us is designed and bred to remain in motion. Our instinctual drives make us tourists, argues Austrian systems analyst Cesare Marchetti. He believes that it is among the most basic of human drives to explore the furthest reaches of surrounding territory and to return with tales—and souvenirs to prove the stories are true. Furthermore, this drive is remarkably stable over time and across countries in the developed world. Whether in Europe, North America, or Asia, now or fifty years ago, people spend about 13 percent of their disposable income on travel.

Of course, most of the trips people take are quite mundane affairs—business excursions that are hardly memorable; long weekends that, while enjoyable and uplifting, are not especially memorable;

two-week vacations as part of tour groups, producing memories that quickly fade. Yet very occasionally in your life, you do have an experience while on the road that is reminiscent of the most noble explorers before you, an experience that forever changes your life.

HERO'S JOURNEY

All our greatest stories are about a quest, whether to find Oz, Canterbury, Tibet, Mecca, the Holy Grail, or the Promised Land. Travelers are revered for their courage and their chutzpah. Moses, James Cook, Marco Polo, Ferdinand Magellan, Christopher Columbus, Lewis and Clark, Neil Armstrong—these very names stoke our imaginations.

Through his studies of mythology throughout the ages, Joseph Campbell identified recurrent themes that have been prevalent in all human cultures. Whether among the Eskimos or Arapaho, ancient Greeks or Incas, Maoris or Irish, people tell a similar story of the hero's journey. This universal legend is the story of a hero who is called by chance to undertake some adventure, an invitation that is initially refused. As everyone knows, such journeys to slay dragons or find the Holy Grail are fraught with danger; besides, the hero isn't all that certain he or she would like to be transformed.

In spite of fears and apprehensions, the hero is persuaded to begin the journey, almost always alone. Supernatural aid is provided, however, in the form of advice or amulets from a guardian such as Merlin or a fairy godmother. It's a good thing, too, because there are always trials and obstacles to overcome.

It is through the confrontation with tests along the road that the hero finds his or her true nature. By surviving the ordeals of the trip, the hero becomes stronger, wiser, more poised and confident. And this goes far beyond the spoils of victory—the gold or crown the hero gains.

This most popular mythological tale, told around the world for ages, is the story of transformative travel. Every cultural group pays homage to the courageous journey, the one undertaken not only to save the community, but to save oneself. It was recognized, long before psychotherapy was ever invented, that the best way to promote growth and healing was to take a trip, to go in search of adventure. This phenomenon still operates today.

In the aftermath of eight climbers dying on Mount Everest in 1996, all in a single storm, journalists and moralists alike wondered if something was seriously wrong that even amateurs could pay lots of money to be escorted to the top of the world. Sandy Hill Pittman, a New York socialite who was one of the very few who reached the summit and lived to tell about it, remarked to her critics that the risks were well worth the gain. In fact, a Himalayan trek was "cheaper and more satisfying than a New York shrink." Her words exactly.

Although in the telling of the myths and stories, audiences are generally more impressed with the external rewards that accrue to the traveler—fame, riches, and symbols of achievement (souvenirs)—it is really the inner rewards that are more lasting. Fame is fleeting. Property is lost. Riches are squandered. But wisdom and serenity are yours forever.

The Universal Metaphor of Change

All of this can be yours, it is told, if you are willing to venture forth into the unknown. Historian Daniel Boorstein, author of several volumes about the great explorers, describes travel—the movement through space, whether by land, sea, or air—as the universal metaphor for change. He laments further that modern life has made the noble journey more or less a thing of the past. Just as travel has become more convenient, comfortable, affordable, accessible, so too has it lost some of its confusion, unpredictability, danger, even terror. Whereas once upon a time, the simple act of visiting a neighboring settlement was considered a major enterprise in which you could encounter unforeseen discoveries, bandits, predators, battles in progress, starvation, nowadays we measure the success of a trip according to whether all goes according to plan. Further, we carefully construct our plans in such a way that we can exercise maximum control at every point. We even board airplanes according to our assigned seat numbers.

———

The hero's journey is a story of transformative travel that replaces the present and past with a different future. New patterns and possibilities emerge. Many of your most cherished beliefs about life, and your unique role in it, come into question. When your trip comes to an end, your journey is just beginning. Now you must consider exactly where you have been heading and whether that's truly where you want to go. You are at a turning point, a place where new paths make themselves known.

The trip usually takes place at a time in your life when you are looking for your own Holy Grail—some dissatisfaction or hunger that you are longing to confront. If the journey is successful, you return a changed person, a hero in your own eyes.

2

Why People Travel

$\mathcal{T}$ravel evolved throughout the ages, as we have seen, from an activity that was undertaken primarily for commercial or territorial purposes to an experience that involves altruistic, aesthetic, recreational, and educational motives. Before you examine exactly what you might be looking for in your next adventure, let's review the various reasons people undertake journeys that are often stressful and certainly costly.

We begin with the story of a transformative trip of my own, which occurred many years ago and actually planted the first seeds for this book. Embedded in the narrative are elements that are common to many trips that change people's lives in dramatic ways.

A PERSONAL JOURNEY

When I was a lad of twenty-three, I felt like a wreck. My life already seemed over. The future ahead appeared as much like a wasteland as the emptiness I could see looking over my shoulder at the past. I felt lost, without choices, without hope.

I was stuck in a job that I hated and trapped in an engagement with a woman I didn't love. At the time, both commitments seemed like a good idea but I suppose it was the fantasy of being a successful, married businessman that appealed to me far more than the reality.

My fiancée was hardly a shrew; in fact, she was a lovely woman who made me feel safe and cared for. She knew just what she wanted in life and the role I would play as her escort. The only problem was that I would have to become a person I didn't much like.

The same could be said for my work. I was doing well as a budding young executive, making more money than I could spend, moving up the ladder of success as fast as I could climb. I was learning to be manipulative and ruthless, and to judge my worth solely in terms of the value of my car and my last deal. I didn't care for what I saw in the mirror or what I heard when I listened to myself talk. I was depressed. I felt immobilized. Yet I didn't have a good reason to quit. What would I say to people? How could I explain that I didn't want what I had, even though it was what I always wanted?

It was about this time that I decided to take a class as a lark, just for entertainment value. It happened to be an introductory counseling course, one that involved a fair bit of personal sharing in the group. We were challenged to make commitments publicly about things we would like to change in our lives, and in a moment of pure insanity, I declared that by the next time classmates saw me I was going to quit my job and end my engagement.

A few days later I found myself unemployed and unattached, dizzy with freedom, yet terrified about what to do next. I needed some kind of transition from my old life to a new one, a ritual of sorts that would help me to transform myself from one person into another. So I did something just as impulsive as my previous actions: I booked a trip for a week in Aruba.

In spite of what others might have thought, I was not running away *from* something but *to* something. I wanted a clean break and I knew I needed to get away from my usual environment and influences so as to think clearly about where I was headed.

I made meticulous preparations for my trip—not where I'd go and what I'd do but rather the books I'd read and the tapes I would listen to in order to reprogram myself in a new direction.

Sure enough, once settled into my room on this little island, I began my process of self-change. I really could have been anywhere as long as nobody could reach me by phone and I had the peace and quiet to think about what I wanted to do. I spent the mornings going for long walks on the beach, the afternoons sitting under a favorite divi divi tree reading books and listening to tapes. Probably most important of all, I forced myself to get out of my shell and venture out and meet people. Ordinarily shy, I redefined myself as someone who was perfectly capable of striking up a conversation with anyone I chose. Since nobody knew the "real" me, the way I had always been, I felt free to be someone completely different.

It took me the better part of a year to pay off that trip, but I'm convinced that single week in Aruba was worth three years in therapy. I had been able to transform myself while I was there because of several processes that will be discussed throughout this book:

• *I created a mindset that made me ripe for change.* I expected that big things were on the horizon, that a trip such as this could change my life. I believed with all my heart that I *could* change my life, if only I could find a quiet place to sort things out and experiment with new ways of thinking and acting. One way or the other, I was determined that this experience would transform me.

• *I insulated myself from the usual influences in my life and the people whose approval was most important.* One of the reasons that therapy often takes such a long time is that once you leave the safety and support of a session, you reenter the world where the old cues elicit the familiar reactions. In spite of your best intentions and the proclamations of your family and associates, people often don't want you to change—unless it is according to their specifications. By separating myself from others' approval and influences, I was able to think more clearly about what it was that I really wanted.

• *I structured my time in ways designed to produce change and growth.* Solitude, isolation, or novel environments in themselves are not enough; you must also complete tasks that are therapeutic and educational. The most important part of any therapy is not what you understand or what you talk about, but what you *do*. Insight without action is entertaining but not always helpful.

It would have been my normal pattern to hang out by myself, read escape fiction, and call home regularly to reassure others that I was still the same person who left. Instead, I structured my time in ways that I knew would lead to changes. In my transformative schedule, I had time allocated for each of several different activities that would shake me up a bit.

• *I pushed myself to experiment with new ways of being.* I experimented with some alternative lifestyles. I pretended to be a different person than I usually was. I acted in unfamiliar ways just to see how it felt. Whereas normally I would never have approached a stranger, I forced myself to do that again and again. In other circumstances, when I wanted to congregate with others for the comfort of companionship, I pushed myself to go off alone. Whatever I would usually do in various circumstances, I forced myself to do the opposite. This reinforced the idea to me that anything was possible, that I could do most anything I wanted.

• *I made public commitments of what I intended to do in the future so that it would be harder to back down.* There were times when I wanted to avoid doing those things I found most frightening. Until this trip, I had never traveled to a strange place deliberately alone. Whenever I thought about taking safe routes, I imagined that I would soon have to face my classmates, to whom I felt accountable. For this reason, it helps a lot to declare publicly exactly what you are going to do.

• *I processed my experiences systematically so that I could make sense of what was happening.* It is not what you live but what sense you make of experience that matters most. I wrote in a journal each day. I spoke to people I met about what I was doing and why. I solicited their feedback to find out about the effects of my persona. When I returned, I talked to a number of people I trusted about what had transpired. Each of them offered a different perspective that I valued and found useful in integrating the experience into my life.

• *I instituted changes when I returned in such a way that I kept the momentum going.* It's easier to make changes when you are away from home; the hard part is to maintain the changes after you return. To make sure that I didn't slip back into old patterns, I immediately initiated a number of decisions regarding my work and relationships that forced me to continue moving forward. I had no choice; I couldn't go back.

• *I found ways to build into my daily life the parts of what worked best for me during my travels.* After this week, I realized that I had enjoyed being more assertive and proactive in my life rather than waiting for things to happen. Furthermore, I discovered in a number of little ways that I was capable of doing things that I hadn't considered before. Because I was so terrified that all my effort would be wasted, that I would slip back into the same patterns, I proved to myself again and again that I didn't need to be in Aruba to become a different person.

• *I decided that much of my future traveling would have some transformative dimension to it.* Whereas it's possible to make extraordinary progress in a single week, or even a day, transformative change is something that takes place over a lifetime. I vowed that periodically I would structure refresher trips into my life so that I might be able to continue growing at a rapid pace.

This trip to Aruba was twenty-five years ago. While there have been a few other times since then that I have made dramatic changes in my life as a result of my travel experiences, most of my excursions have been as pedestrian as your own. I've traveled for all the reasons that people usually do so—to escape and bathe myself in luxury, for status and attention, for romance, to seek relief from boredom or stress, to scout new opportunities, to conduct business, to collect things, and not nearly enough for personal growth. It is only in the last few years that I've returned once again to the intentions of my youth, to reclaim the incredible excitement and challenge that comes from transformative travel.

REASONS FOR TRAVELING

I said this book isn't for everyone. Certainly many people are not interested in changing themselves. They already like things the way they are (or are convinced they do), or they admit they aren't up to the task of confronting any major challenges such as those that might be a part of making significant life changes.

I'm not talking here about quitting your job, or getting a divorce, or moving to the South Pacific (although perhaps those *are* desirable changes for some people). Transformative changes don't necessarily alter what you do on the outside, but they produce dramatic alterations in the ways you look at things. Of course, often this does mean you will respond differently to situations where previously you might have behaved in other ways. Much depends on what you are missing, what you are searching for, and what you'd like to do differently.

Clarifying Personal Motives

There are two main reasons why people make changes in their lives—because they *need* to, and because they *want* to. In the first situation, there is something you have to do differently to regain equilibrium. You feel stymied, lost, perhaps even in great pain. You know that unless you change some fundamental things about your life, you will never be happy or satisfied.

In the second case, it is not so much that you are unhappy as you enjoy the growth that comes from stretching yourself in new directions. You like the way it feels to be challenged and stimulated.

Unless you believe in reincarnation, you've got one shot at this life, and that one may already be half over. Each day is a new gift that is yours to use as you like. Unfortunately, it rarely feels that way. There are so many obligations and responsibilities to fulfill, so many people we answer to for our actions, so many commitments we feel we must live up to. Our time rarely feels as if it is our own. From the moment you awake until the moment your head hits the pillow, there are people all day long who want a piece of you. Once you parcel out your time to work obligations, social commitments, family needs, there is precious little left over to indulge yourself in what *you* might really like to do.

This predicament is so depressing that many people don't even want to think about how little control they have over their lives. They never allow themselves to be alone for fear they might have to confront the emptiness of their lives. During those times when they are in their own company, whether in the car or the bathroom, they fill up the silent moments with radio, television, computer, or telephone. Anything to avoid thinking about how little control they really have.

For others, there is quite a different problem. It's not so much that they don't like being alone as they have so few opportunities for solitude. In either case, or anything in between, people feel they have precious little time they can truly call their own. That is what vacation travel is designed to do—to give you the opportunity to get away from your normal obligations so you can replenish yourself. Two, three, four, even six weeks a year is hardly the time you deserve to do what you want with your life.

The object of transformative change ought to be the kind of growth that helps you bring home and make part of you, forever, whatever you learned about yourself while you were gone. These kinds of big changes make your daily life more a holiday in the sense that you derive greater pleasure and fulfillment from those experiences you now take for granted.That is something you can learn from a lecture or a book, or better yet in therapy. You learn it better and quicker, however, when you find yourself in novel situations that force you to develop new resources and respond creatively to challenges you face.

Nowadays, most good therapy takes place not during the sessions but outside in the world where things matter most. It does little good to have perfect insight into why you are troubled if this understanding doesn't lead you to behave in new ways. Therapists are thus continuously devising ways to encourage people to complete tasks that will produce real, transformative changes.

No doubt you've known people who have been in therapy for years. They understand all too well why they are so messed up but you can't see any difference in their behavior. Time and time again, I've heard myself say to clients, it's not what you do with me that matters most but what you do when you're not here. Many therapists, educators, and certainly health insurance companies, agree with this philosophy—the emphasis in today's climate of managed care is to provide brief, efficient, focused treatments that produce immediate and measurable relief of symptoms. While this limited goal is often shortsighted, failing to respond to people's more elusive human need for understanding, and also not addressing underlying issues that may be sparking the present difficulties, it does remind us of how important it is to act as well as to reflect on our lives.

Whether you're interested in making changes to fill some need or to stimulate your life for the enjoyment of growth, travel experiences can provide the ideal structure for personal changes—if you know where you're going and how to get there.

Who Do You Want to Be?

You can decide this moment you'd like to refashion your personality or style, but other people won't let you get away with it. Try announcing to family and friends that you will henceforth be more assertive or playful or passionate and then watch them shake their heads in amusement. Sure. Even if you are serious in following through with your resolve, others won't much like your changes—it means they have to make changes as well to accommodate themselves to your alterations. It is far easier for them to get you to give up your efforts. As the following traveler discovered, dramatic changes are much likelier if you can get away—if you can disconnect yourself from expectations, not only those of others but your own:

I didn't like who I was, nor did I like how other people viewed me. Oh, they saw me as a nice enough fellow, even if not very bright or talented. For so long I accepted this mediocrity. I didn't really consider things could be any different.

Then I saw this ad for a summer course at Harvard, with virtually open admissions. I jumped at the opportunity, thinking that nobody knows me there so I can be someone else. I was scared, of course. Put a lot of pressure on myself to do well.

From the moment I arrived, I took on a new persona. I pretended I was bright. Carried books with me wherever I went. Read them at every opportunity. I talked to people as equals rather than being so deferential and self-effacing as I usually am. I was giddy with the realization that as far as my new friends were concerned, this strange person they knew as me really was a part of me I didn't know existed.

The hard part was coming home. I thought for sure I'd revert back to my old ways. I figured my family and people who had known me my whole life would never accept me as a bright, confident, capable person. To some extent, this is true. Even after many years there are those who refuse to see me except as I was. The important thing, though, is that I learned that I could be whoever I wanted. But the only way I could have figured that out was to get away from everyone and everything that was familiar. I had to start over fresh. I had to be around people who didn't know the way I was supposed to be.

It is one of the most fascinating phenomena of human nature that people are so threatened by change that they will sometimes do anything to stop it. If you doubt this, try losing weight, stopping smoking, starting an exercise program, and note the subtle and direct ways people may try to sabotage you. Because if you succeed, it means they no longer have an excuse for their own procrastination.

That's why people often have to run away from home, so to speak, before they can make radical changes in lifestyle. That's why inpatient alcohol units, week-long retreats, or health camps are often successful, at least in the short run. They are designed to take people away from their usual environments, to reprogram new habits based on healthier cues. The same can be said for transformative travel. When you get away from the people and places and cues that normally influence your behavior, you are free to make new decisions on how you'd like to respond in the future.

KINDS OF TRAVEL

Ask someone planning a journey about the reasons for the trip and you are likely to hear an answer that involves escaping winter weather, visiting friends or relatives, relieving stress and boredom, attending a special event like a wedding, or conducting business. Yet these are only the reasons people *say* they travel, and are usually not at all the real motives behind their actions.

People travel for an assortment of reasons. They wish to fulfill something missing in their lives. They feel more creative in strange places. They want to show friends and neighbors how prosperous they are. They indulge in a secret life in which they are able to engage in forbidden behavior only when they are away from home. They collect trophies in the same way a big game hunter mounts animals on the wall.

Here are some of the many reasons people travel:

TYPE	PURPOSE	EXAMPLES
Exile	redemption and penance	Adam and Eve, Lawrence of Arabia
Heroic	testing one's resources	Charles Lindbergh, Robert Perry
Adventurous	physical challenges	Edmund Hillary, Robert Scott
Anthropological	immersion in a culture	Margaret Mead
Spiritual	communion with God or nature	Buddha, Moses
Pilgrimage	purification, honoring dead	Visitors to Lourdes, Jerusalem
Retreat	isolation and reflection	Henry Thoreau
Conquest	territorial expansion	Napoleon, Alexander the Great
Exploration	mapping new territory	James Cook, Lewis and Clark
Nomadic	relocation for better living	Plains Indians, Aboriginals, Migrant farm workers
Scientific	systematic observation	Charles Darwin, Carl Linnaeus
Literary	expand consciousness	Mark Twain, Robert Louis Stevenson
Commercial	engage in trade	Marco Polo
Tourism	amusement and distraction	Visitors to Disney World, Las Vegas

To some extent, transformative travel can and does include any or all of the motives just mentioned. However, people driven to explore the outer reaches of the planet and themselves are primarily motivated by intellectual curiosity, emotional containment or elaboration, or physical challenge. More likely, a combination of two or more of these motives plays a predominant role.

I Think, Therefore I Travel

Intellectual curiosity is favored by those who are mostly in their heads rather than their hearts. Such individuals are logical, analytic, and intensely interested in learning about many aspects of the world. They are history buffs, bird watchers, respecters of flora and fauna, collectors of rare items. They frequent museums and really study the exhibits. They do extensive research about the places they visit, not only in standard guidebooks, but in other literature that informs them about geographic, cultural, and economic facets of their destinations.

People whose travels are motivated by intellectual curiosity tend be bright and inquisitive. They may be frustrated by aspects of their jobs that don't provide the kind of stimulation they crave. Travel satisfies a strong need to exercise their brains, a kind of candy for the mind and senses.

Intellectual curiosity can be a powerful motive to promote personal growth. When you change the way you think about yourself, you also change your feelings and reactions. When you alter your understanding of the world, and the way things fit together, every other part of your being may soon follow.

For example, Monty is in the construction business. He is used to working not only with his hands, but also with his brain—figuring costs, planning projects, cutting expenses, looking for ways to find investors. Monty reads avidly and really enjoys talking to people, most anyone, about anything—politics, education, the Punic Wars, whatever comes up. Although he enjoys his work and his life in general, Monty finds that daily reality never comes close to the more exciting times he has read about in historical fiction. Travel serves for him as an outlet to exercise his brain.

If Ph.D.'s were given for life experience, Monty would have a string of letters after his name. He just returned from a week-long visit to Washington, D.C., practically all of which he spent roaming around the Smithsonian's assorted halls and galleries. His head is filled with things he learned and his confidence is brimming. He will tell you anything you ever wanted to know about the formation of rocks or the mating habits of the sloth.

Monty, you see, never finished high school—but he lives in a world in which his investors, partners, customers, and friends are all college graduates, if not MBAs. Travel has been his schooling, the way he has educated himself on a par with his peers. His trips have transformed him from an awkward, unmotivated, unsuccessful student to a poised, confident, worldly, and articulate professional. After returning from each trip, Monty feels a little bit wiser, and also more at peace with himself. Yes, he still talks too much, still feels compelled to prove that he's as bright and capable as his college-educated peers. But he is learning, ever so slowly, that wisdom is never attained in school so much as on the road.

Deep in Your Heart

By contrast, emotional containment and elaboration describe those who are open to changing on a feeling level rather than through their intellect. This could either be for situational reasons, such as undergoing a life transition (graduation, child leaving home, midlife crisis) or a critical incident (divorce, job change, death of loved one). In addition, people who are traveling in a way that speaks to their hearts may do so not for any specific reason but rather because it is part of their preferred style.

There are distinct gender differences that often divide us into two subgroups within this category of travelers. Typically, men tend to be more emotionally restrained while women are far more expressive. There are good reasons for this, evolutionarily speaking. In a previous book, *The Language of Tears,* I described how men receive strong biological as well as cultural imperatives to withhold any inadvertent cues that might give a competitor an advantage that might be useful during combat or competition over resources and potential mates. Women, on the other hand, are superhuman as a rule in terms of emotional sensitivity and fluency. They are experts in the language of tears—both reading and expressing them over time. Emotions have evolved as a kind of weapon for women, or at least a tool that allows them to get their needs met in a world where superior physical strength and speed have historically dominated.

What all this means is that men are often so guarded with their feelings they become emotionally constipated. Travel is an opportunity for such overcontrolled individuals of both genders to break out of the shell of emotional containment. Likewise, some people (most often women) struggle not only with problems of expressing emotions but restraining them as well. They feel out of control. In mild cases, they are merely annoyed with themselves because their feelings get the best of them. In more serious cases, sleep, eating patterns, and daily functioning may be disrupted.

In both instances of travel style, emotion is the heart of the matter—the need to regain some control during a period of disequilibrium, to reignite passion and excitement, or to feed a continual desire for emotional stimulation. The latter case is described by one woman who is not only comfortable with her high degree of emotional fluency but is proud of the courage it takes to lead with her heart: "Sunsets make me cry. I see little children in the streets, I want to take them home with me. I feel raw when I'm traveling, whether I'm alone or with my husband who is quite different than I am. Everything is so much closer to the bone. I feel everything more intensely, which sometimes drives my husband batty, but really I think he likes it."

Both women and men travel to stimulate themselves emotionally, but also to chill out from overstimulation. The greatest urge is to shut down feelings, temporarily, because things are feeling out of control. Lorian Hemingway visited a monastery to escape the noise and chaos of her life. Upon arrival, she was asked a simple question: "What is it that you seek here?"

"I first thought of a tightrope walker poised above an abyss, the way I'd been when I arrived. Then I thought of the way I'd felt standing solidly on the path that went through the woods of the compound, of the calm that enveloped me as I listened to the wind, watched the deer, heard the bell ring in the chapel. That sort of balance. And I hoped I would take a portion of this place back with me as a reminder—to slow down, to breathe, to seek balance."

Of course, hoping to take the best part of what you learned during a trip is not nearly enough. It takes far more than mere resolution to initiate changes that become enduring. It is for this reason that some people seek a different sort of adventure that bypasses both the heart and head, going right to the body and soul.

Physical Challenges

Adventure-based traveling appeals, most often, to the human need for new challenges. People often find that they can be profoundly affected when they are engaged in activities that push them to new limits.

Travel centered on adventures, especially those that are highly structured, is designed to change people by teaching them new skills, allowing them to practice in safe environments, and then to meet a challenge that appears to be beyond reach. Instructors then help participants to process their experiences, make sense of what they learned about themselves, and apply the concepts to other areas of their lives.

People often return from such trips profoundly changed. Yet when you ask them what happened, they babble on about these horrifying things they did and disgusting things they ate. They talk about the pain they suffered. They show you scars and blisters. They tell you stories of avalanches, sleepless nights, and using snow for toilet paper. And through it all, they are smiling like angels.

What the hell happened to them, you ask. The answer is that they were shaken to their very core. They accomplished things they didn't know they could do. They raised their tolerances for pain and discomfort. They developed intense, mutually supportive relationships in a brief period of time. They drew on inner resources that had long been dormant. Finally, they thought *and* felt a lot about where they had been, where they are now, and where they are headed. No wonder they seem so different.

Long before we ever created structured programs to promote change through physical challenge, people traveled for very personal reasons to deal with their demons. Meriwether Lewis was subject to periodic bouts of depression, probably a victim of a full-fledged manic depression. In addition, according to his biographer Stephen Ambrose, he was also prone to hypochondria and may very well have been an active alcoholic. Yet in spite of these severe mental disorders, Lewis was able to redeem himself through his travels.

If ever there was a transformative expedition, certainly Lewis's journey with William Clark and thirty companions across the breadth of North America qualifies. There is nothing like feeling productive to overcome one's personal problems. In a little over two years, Lewis and company discovered a hundred new animals and another two hundred plants unknown to science. He constructed the first map of the continent, collected specimens of various rocks and creatures, negotiated treaties with Indian tribes, faced starvation, floods, disease, grizzly bears, hostile Sioux and Blackfeet. He got shot, he climbed mountain ranges, he walked and rowed eight thousand miles—and in so doing, he transformed himself into one of the most capable leaders of all time. Of course, once he stopped traveling and stayed in one place for a while, his melancholia got the best of him; Lewis eventually killed himself.

In the case of Meriwether Lewis, travel changed him only as long as he remained in motion. The primary motive for him, as it is for many others in less extreme form, was to distract himself from other problems over which he felt little control.

ALTERED STATES OF CONSCIOUSNESS

One woman, interviewed by Gully Wells about the nature of travel as an addiction, speaks about the experience as a strange sensual, even sexual obsession in which the more you get, the more you want: "I know it's ridiculous, but I am just as excited to go to Boston as to Timbuktu. From the moment you arrive in a foreign place, every sense is heightened. Sight, smell, touch, hearing. . . . Part of it is superficial, but it still excites me."

Wells describes travel as a kind of drug, an altered state of consciousness in which you are transported not only to another place, but another dimension. Your senses are intensified. Your hearing and vision are hypersensitive. Every sound, smell, and sensation takes over your whole being. This is all part of the magic of travel. There is no other human activity that has greater potential to alter your perceptions or the ways you choose to run your life.

Acting Out Fantasies

Travel is an antidote for boredom. And the truth is that most people are bored with aspects of their lives. We find our daily routines tedious and uninteresting. We take our primary relationships for granted. Conversations at mealtimes are less than stimulating. Work is, well, *work* much of the time.

It is a grind driving in rush-hour traffic. We frequent the same restaurants, by and large, and order basically the same things. Our social lives follow predictable routines, our family lives even more so. Our days are rigidly structured, more so than we ever realize. From the moment we open our eyes in the morning, we function on auto-pilot—brush our teeth in the usual pattern, dress ourselves in the familiar order, go to work along the same pathways, even talk about the same things during interludes with friends and colleagues.

While these routines and familiar patterns are comforting to a certain degree, even enjoyable in their familiar pleasures, they also make us feel deprived of stimulation. That is where travel comes in as a life-altering experience—its basic function is to change our environment. During vacations, we move at a different pace. We experiment with alternative roles. We try different foods, engage in unusual activities, free ourselves from routines that are most familiar.

Certainly it doesn't take long to develop new repetitive patterns—go on strolls in the evenings, read the morning paper on the balcony, lie out on the beach under a favorite tree—but until these new routines become boring, we end up trying out a number of new behaviors and activities that are really quite enjoyable.

We hear strange accents and novel sounds in the streets. The food tastes different, and especially the smells all around us cry out for our attention. We see people acting in strange, often incomprehensible ways. We are bombarded by new sights and sensations, all of which act to transport us to another world. Literally.

In a classic study of leisure behavior, French sociologist Joffre Dumazedier described this sort of escape that takes place during travel as a "secondary reality," one in which fantasies may be acted out. The appeal of cruises and resorts, for instance, is the way they pamper you, let you live in a fantasy world for a week or two and pretend to be part of the leisure class with nothing better to do than decide what to eat and whether to take a nap, a walk, or go shopping. You pretend you are rich as you sip piña coladas on your private veranda watching the sunset, or a naturalist as you forage through the woods studying plant life and bird sounds, or a champion surfer as you play on the waves.

One of the things that is unique about travel, at least for adults, is that it takes place in a world of fantasy and play. Under such circumstances, you willingly suspend normal boundaries of reality to take on alternative roles of make-believe. In their book on marketing techniques for travel agents, Edward Mayo and Lance Jarvis remind the profession that they are essentially selling people's dreams. They use outdoor recreation as one example of this fantasy world, a set of activities that, once scrutinized closely, seem ridiculous in modern life.

Take camping and backpacking, for example. Although people live in comfortable homes equipped with all modern conveniences, they choose to venture out in the wilderness and pretend to live off the land. They engage in "symbolic labor"—chopping wood, tracking, fishing, hunting—all reminiscent of our ancestral past. In a sense, they pretend they are living in the past for a while when they isolate themselves in this way. Behavior tends to regress to a more basic level. People become more natural about their body functions. Conversations take on a more raucous, uninhibited flavor. And yet all this is a game of make-believe in which the participants use travel to change their usual environment dramatically. This creates unique conditions, likely to produce novel experiences that are remembered.

There is nothing intrinsically significant about wilderness travel that produces major changes. If someone who lived regularly in that world visited a city, he or she would be just as affected by an environment that appeared unique. While on a flight between two Australian cities, I sat next to an Aboriginal mother and youngster who had obviously never flown before. They were barefoot and spoke little English, a circumstance that made communication between us challenging. They seemed little concerned about the extraordinary view out the window of the plane—perhaps the very concept of flying was more than they could handle at the time. But they were utterly spellbound by the folding tray table that I showed them how to unlatch from the seat in front of them. All through the trip they kept taking the table up and down, up and down, giggling the whole time. The headphones provided them even more amusement. What seemed so ordinary to me was amazing to them. What makes a trip particularly memorable is its uniqueness in your experience.

Healing and Peace

One effect of travel is a change in scenery, and that is often just the antidote you need during times when life seems to be unraveling all around you. A woman whose husband had recently died found herself losing her sense of reality: "My life with my husband had started to feel like it had been a dream. Had I only imagined it all? I needed to come to terms with my life we had shared when he was so suddenly taken away from me."

While therapy is often one solution for those struggling to find their way—as are less constructive options like alcohol or withdrawal—this woman decided to use travel as a way to heal herself. Her plan was to revisit some of the places she had once shared with her husband. "Experiencing the sights, sounds, smells, the people, allowed me to rekindle feelings that had begun to fade. I was able to wallow in these sensations, and eventually, to set them aside. This helped me to bring closure with some issues I had been struggling with."

Just as people might travel to heal themselves, they might also use trips to see themselves from a different vantage point. This is just what one man had in mind while struggling to find some sort of accommodation with his current life; he was stuck in the past. "Raspberries, wildflowers, and gorgeous trees surrounded the Indiana house where I grew up. My friends lived nearby and the whole setup was idyllic. After my Dad died, we had to sell the house and move away. That place, my childhood home, took on a magical quality in my dreams. Nothing has ever satisfied me since then."

After twenty years, this man was consistently unhappy with his life and his circumstances. His thoughts kept returning to his childhood home and how that was the only place he could ever feel content. Finally, he decided to confront the fantasy by going back to his home town.

"I was anticipating a miracle. The reality hit me pretty quickly. I had little in common with the people I had once grown up with. The town seemed squalid, the house and surroundings no longer resembled what I had once imagined them to be."

At first he was devastated. After all, this was the death of a lifelong dream. Now what was left him?

"While I was in Indiana I came to a momentous realization that I really did like myself! I liked my life! I had become the person I was specifically because I had left my home. My eyes were opened to the realities of my life in a way that could not have occurred if I had not ventured out of my familiar surroundings in search of answers."

Healing and peace often result from a new perspective on things, one that emerges on a journey. After his wife died of cancer, Peter Mattheissen went in search of the legendary snow leopard of the Himalayas. This was a pilgrimage for him, "a journey of the heart." Like anyone who has visited a Third World country, he found that he couldn't look at what he saw, and yet he couldn't look away. "In India, human misery seems so pervasive that one takes in only stray details; a warped leg or a dead eye, a sick pariah dog eating withered grass, an ancient woman lifting her sari to move her shrunken bowels by the road." His own pain seemed dwarfed by comparison.

Only by getting away from our daily lives, and immersing ourselves in another world, can we fully grasp the senseless complaining that we do about our own annoyances. We whine about the promotion that passed us by, the catty remark by a coworker. We worry incessantly about paying off the credit cards or how we will put together enough money to buy the house or car or boat we really want. We obsess about our hair turning gray or falling out, about our bodies aging before we are ready. We rehearse over and over again the things we wished we had said, or the things we intend to do next.

All the while you are in this reverie, you are walking through the streets of Port au Prince, Calcutta, Manila, or Lima. There are people starving to death before your eyes, people who would kill for a pair of shoes. You distance yourself from this misery; it is too much to bear, too far removed from your experience.

Yet it is exactly this type of environment that jars you sufficiently to consider alternative ways of viewing your life, where you have been, and where you are headed next. Travel can therefore be a way to find some sort of peace when everything else you have tried doesn't work.

Entertainment and Indulgence

People are motivated not only to confront their fantasies but also to indulge them. There is something to be said for uncomplicated fun—and many trips are motivated primarily by the pursuit of pleasure, if not decadence. Some people will indulge themselves in the lap of luxury for a week. Others venture to Thailand to engage in sexual escapades or sign on to a cruise ship for a romantic fling. Sometimes, people are even satisfied with illusions of grandeur; they will travel in a world of fantasy.

In a scathing look at my own city, Michael Ventura puzzles about why people choose to visit Las Vegas during their vacations. Ordinarily quite frugal about the ways they spend their money, people will literally flush their hard-earned dollars down the throat of a machine, knowing they will probably not win. Furthermore, the grim, fatalistic expression on their faces shows fairly clearly they are not having a very good time.

It seems only fair to pick on my own home town as the seat of tremendous plasticity, superficiality, manipulation, and yes, despair. After all, it is one of the two most popular tourist destinations in the world. The other, of course, is Disney World, and I would contend that it is really not all that different from Vegas. Both travel spots are designed to provide a predictable experience in an efficient, factory-like setting disguised in illusions and images. They are both in the business of entertainment.

Of course, you hardly need a theme park or casino-resort to entertain or indulge yourself. The very act of travel can be awfully self-liberating, as one person explains:

> I experience exhilaration when I travel. All the baggage is left behind and I can create any persona I wish at any moment. This is great fun! There is no rule that dictates I have to tell the truth about myself. I can explore various roles, and I do. I find this *so* therapeutic.
>
> The roles I take on while traveling can vary from day to day and place to place, or I may maintain a single role for an entire trip. I create fantasies in my mind and have the chance to transform them into a kind of reality. Strange as it might seem, this is how I find my own sanity.
>
> I am often running away from something when I travel. Nothing serious, really, just a depressed mood, failed financial transaction, troubled relationship, and so on. I use travel as a way to distract myself for a while, but also to engage myself more fully in what is possible.

It is probably apparent from this last set of observations that only part of our motives are actually visible to us. We may think we are traveling for one reason, that is, to indulge or entertain ourselves, when we are actually on the road for other reasons that are beyond our immediate awareness.

Hidden Motives

Sometimes you undertake journeys not so much for yourself but on behalf of others. You may not even be aware, consciously, why you are driven to visit a special place or conquer a particular challenge. William Willis was one such traveler; he spent his life from the age of fifteen tackling progressively more difficult voyages at sea. He sailed by raft alone from Peru to Australia, then from England to North America. He eventually was lost at sea off the coast of Iceland some time during his seventy-fifth year.

When asked why he made such hazardous voyages, Willis once admitted that he wasn't sure if he was fulfilling his own dream to pursue solitude at sea: "Ever since I was a child at my mother's knee, I heard her speak of the beauty of open fields and woods and the wise and endless sea. Truly a dreamer and seer she was, for then she had only known the sea from pictures. And so I am just walking her way."

Think about whose dreams you live for. Consider the legacies of your parents, and your ancestors before them, who have been subtly, perhaps overtly, pushing you toward journeys that you may take on their behalf.

—⁓—

Recreational travel is ordinarily conceived of as a form of leisure activity, along with other diversions both passive (television, spectator sports, reading) and active (athletics, hobbies, gardening). When people are asked about why they engage in these things, they ordinarily mention that they help them to relax, to escape from routines, and to allow them freedom to do whatever they want.

Likewise, travel is usually thought of in similar terms: it provides "time outs" from usual responsibilities and supplies a degree of stimulation and excitement that could not be possible otherwise. It is therefore somewhat rare to think about uses of travel to promote self-esteem, self-confidence, well-being in the same sense in which you might consult a psychologist or personal trainer.

Travel, at least the kind we are investigating, represents more than discretionary time in which you can do what you want when you want. While that is certainly therapeutic in itself, taking a trip is a physical act of movement and relocation—not only from place to place but from one state of mind to another.

3

Where Are You Going?

*A*ny journey begins with considerable reflection about where you want to go and how you intend to get there. The kind of trip you might plan will depend on the particular type of change you're after. If your interest is in refashioning the way you look, your priorities might include attention to diet, beefing up or slimming down, a new wardrobe, or a tan. If you are more interested in changing the emotional tempo of your life, you will structure things in such a way that can influence your mood and disposition. Likewise, if you are most concerned with deepening your relationships with loved ones you might arrange a trip designed to promote greater intimacy. So, where you go depends on exactly what you are searching for.

WHAT DO YOU WANT TO TRANSFORM?

Depending on exactly what you're looking for, you'll structure quite different travel plans. Some people are searching for more excitement in their lives, bored with the usual routines and predictable patterns that control their behavior. Others have too much pressure and stress in their lives; they need to find greater peace and tranquility.

Seeking Peace of Mind

Louellen was a busy, overworked sales representative who was also juggling her roles as mother, wife, daughter to ailing parents, and social organizer for her family and friends. Whereas her husband, Mark, felt the need to continuously push the limits of adventure-oriented activities from mountain biking to rock climbing, Louellen felt she had altogether too much excitement in her life—what she longed for was greater peace. Her sleep was often disrupted with head-spinning plans about what she might do to improve her sales figures or how she would care for her parents as their health continued to deteriorate. She was not eating properly, nor taking care of herself nearly as well as she was ministering to the needs of her family and clients.

When it came time for Louellen and Mark to plan for an upcoming vacation, they realized how different their agendas were. Mark wanted to take the whole family to a Club Med where each of them might partake in the staggering assortment of activities available. They could take scuba lessons, go parasailing or river rafting, then at night they could socialize with people from all over the world. "Doesn't that sound great, honey?" Mark enthusiastically spread out the color brochures, his eyes alight with the unlimited possibilities.

Louellen, however, had a different sort of holiday in mind, one that might help her regain control over a life that felt as if it was spinning chaotically wherever forces pulled her. The prospect of being in an environment where people expected her to stay constantly in motion hardly sounded like a welcome break. She would just be trading appointments with clients for a hectic schedule of volleyball, trapeze flying, and cocktail parties.

When Mark asked her what she would most enjoy, Louellen was surprised to hear herself blurt out that she'd love to be locked in a monastery. There would be time to rest and think. No distractions of television, telephones, faxes, and her computer. No clients, children, parents, or husband to take care of. She'd be able just to think about her life and where she was headed. She could sort out what was really most important to her from the daily chores that kept her so busy she had no time for reflection.

"So, why don't you go to a monastery then, if that's what you really want?" Mark seemed serious. "I'll take the kids with me to Club Med. I'll find someone to stay with your parents. You find a mountaintop to sit on where you can eat brown rice, mutter 'ohmmmm' to yourself, or whatever you do at a monastery."

Louellen did exactly that. Rather than traveling halfway around the world to Tibet, she found a retreat center just outside the city where she lived. She spent a week doing nothing but sleeping and eating simple meals whenever she felt like it. Without a watch, or any schedule to follow, she did whatever she liked. She went for long walks. She meditated. And for a whole week she neither heard nor spoke a single word.

Under such circumstances, perhaps you're not the least surprised to find that Louellen returned from her internal travels a bit different from before she left. She felt refreshed and invigorated. She felt resolved to make some changes in her life that might continue the new spirit that had been awakened.

Louellen's family? Oh, they had a great time. Played in the surf. Partied day and night. But it wasn't change they were after.

Acting out of Character

Whereas Louellen's story is one in which she immersed herself in a different environment that allowed her to think, feel, and react in novel ways, such a total shift is rarely necessary. The simple act of leaving home is sometimes enough for many people to act out of their usual roles.

Madeleine, for example, is ordinarily very eager to please. She has played the roles of adoring daughter, dutiful wife, doting mother, and loyal employee all her life. If you asked people who know Madeleine best what she is like, you would hear the word sweet mentioned again and again. Indeed she *is* sweet in the best sense of meaning essentially kind and considerate. Still, if there is one problem that has plagued her throughout her life, it has been taking such good care of others that she sometimes neglects herself. She is reluctant to assert herself and rarely participates in conflict.

Perhaps that is why her husband Wayne was so shocked by what he had just witnessed. They had just arrived at the airport of their destination, weary and irritable. After claiming their luggage, they walked outside to find a taxi where an airport guard pointed to a spot they should stand. As they proceeded to the appointed station, they overheard the guard yelling at them to stand somewhere else; apparently they had at first misunderstood him. Just as they adjusted their position, they once again heard the man yelling at them.

Madeleine had had quite enough. She calmly walked up to him, and in a voice that neither she nor her husband had ever heard before, she told him she thought he was really rude and there was no call to scream at people. If this was how people in his city treated newcomers, it was a wonder anyone ever came back.

The guard looked at her like an insect he debated about whether to squash or not. "Look, lady, are you deaf or something? Just get out of the way and let me do my job."

"You, sir, are not a very nice person, nor are you particularly helpful." With that, Madeleine turned and strode away with a determination her husband had never seen before.

Whatever made her act that way, so out of character? How is it that a woman could spend her life so willing to please others, to avoid conflict at all costs, and then all of a sudden erupt into an assertive spokesperson for the traveling downtrodden?

Actually, several factors were at work. Madeleine was tired and vulnerable, her nerves stretched tight. Also, her husband had not been feeling well. Whereas normally he would take care of everything, his relative docility throughout the journey stimulated Madeleine to take a more active role. Most of all, however, it was being away from her usual environment, the normal cues and obligations, the people and schedules that ruled her life, that permitted her the freedom to be someone different.

The crucial question is now whether this will be an isolated incident, a one-shot burst of inspiration that will quickly fade once Madeleine resumes her usual role and demeanor. Perhaps she will maintain the momentum throughout the trip, continuing to experiment with a new, assertive persona, only to relinquish it after she returns. Maybe this single incident will spark a whole new way of being for her, transforming her into someone more committed to standing up for herself against perceived injustice. One thing is for certain, regardless of how permanent the behavior becomes, this would not have happened at home.

WHAT DO YOU WANT FOR YOUR MONEY?

When you book a trip, what are you actually buying for your money? You may dicker for an hour with a shopkeeper over the price of a trinket, but walk away if you can't get that extra $2 discount. Then, later that same day, you may fork out $100 for a thirty-minute helicopter ride. You'll save the price of a meal by munching complimentary appetizers at a social function, proud of your frugality. Then you'll pay double the legitimate price for a souvenir T-shirt.

The paradoxes are even more pronounced when you look at the bigger picture. People routinely save their money all year long, making sacrifices, doing without things they need, even dipping into retirement holdings or going into debt, and then spend the equivalent of a month's wages or more for a single week on holiday. There's nothing wrong with this choice for allocating limited resources, except that we apply different rules for spending money when traveling than we do during ordinary times. That, after all, is the point of the exercise.

The critical decision, however, is that with limited time and funds available, what do you want for your money? There are a number of factors to consider:

• *Novelty versus familiarity.* In the former, you will eat a cuisine you've never tried before, fully aware that you might not like it. Or you may order pizza, reasonably certain about what you'll get.

• *Simplicity versus indulgence.* Compare the appeal of a stay in a log cabin in the wilderness, with no running water or indoor plumbing, versus a stay in a five-star resort.

• *Hardship versus convenience.* There's a direct connection between what you invest in an experience (or a relationship) and what you get out of it. People often find that a difficult journey helps them to appreciate more what they've discovered when they get there.

• *Submergence versus efficiency.* There are different things possible when you have a month to travel as opposed to a long weekend. That's not to say longer is necessarily better. You could stay at a health spa for three weeks and not change a whit on the inside even if you firmed up on the outside. Likewise, you can work wonders in a single afternoon if you structure your time properly. Still, if time is short you have to do things at a pace different from that of a more extended visit.

• *Single versus multidimensional change.* There are a number of ways you can change—physically, emotionally, morally, spiritually, socially, or intellectually. Depending on the domains you are most interested in, you might plan things in ways to emphasize one type of experience or another.

• *Solo versus accompaniment.* While there are distinct advantages to traveling by yourself, it is usually preferable for most people to go with a partner. It is simply more enjoyable to be in the company of someone you trust and love, to share adventures together, to support one another along the way. You would structure a different sort of trip if you were going alone than you would with someone else, since in most cases your needs would be somewhat different.

• *Amusement versus growth.* It is possible to travel in such a way that you are both entertained and stimulated. (Indeed, none of these polarities are really mutually exclusive.) Nevertheless, you would probably do things a bit differently if your first priority is fun rather than work. And make no mistake about it: transformative travel often involves a lot of work. After all, in many cases you are giving up that which is most comfortable and familiar in favor of situations and circumstances that challenge your endurance, patience, and tolerance.

What Kind of Traveler Are You?

There are not only different kinds of trips that people take for different reasons, but also distinct ways that people prefer to travel. In a study of personality traits associated with various modes of travel, the Canadian government found that among its citizens there were major differences among those who travel actively during vacations and those who don't. The active travelers tend to be more sociable, confident, and curious, whereas the latter group is more restrained, passive, and serious.

Clearly, it takes a certain amount of courage and inquisitiveness to spend your time, energy, and money in search of new experiences. Confirming the Canadian study, as well as other psychological investigations of personality types and preferences, researcher Stanley Plog discovered many years ago that people fall into two main categories. *Psychocentrics* demand predictability in their lives. They travel to familiar places and prefer structured tours with relatively low activity levels. They also stay in traditional tourist accommodations and like relaxing settings free of intrusions or stress. They prefer to have decisions made for them and would not be attracted to life-altering experiences.

By contrast, *allocentrics* like unpredictability. Their flexibility, high energy, and natural curiosity lead them to explore new territory. They prefer a more basic sort of accommodation, rather than insulated luxury, that allows them to interact more with foreign cultures and people. They look for exotic and unusual destinations that provide opportunities for learning, stimulation, and growth.

Among allocentrics are several distinct groups noted by social psychologist Philip Pearce in his study of tourist behavior. As opposed to types he refers to as the "tourist," "holiday maker," "jet-setter," and "business person," who are all interested in controlling their amount of contact with the world they are visiting, allocentric types are less interested in souvenirs and more interested in experimenting with local customs and interacting with host people.

As you would expect, the "conservationist" is interested in the environment, mostly as an observer. This would be similar to the "explorer" who shares a fascination with the land but in a more active role, taking physical risks. The "missionary" is far more interested in local people than in geography, traveling at the most basic level and searching for the meaning of life rather than souvenirs or photographs. The "hippie" also prefers the simplest mode of travel, but cares more about personal pleasures than about growth.

Each of these types, and however you classify yourself, depends on the particular role-related behaviors that motivate you most. Are you more interested in people or places? Do you like to visit famous places or those in remote regions? Do you prefer luxury or simplicity when you travel? Do you take physical risks? Are you inclined to experiment with local foods and customs? Are you seeking sensual, ethereal, or cerebral pleasures? Do you like to stay in one place or see as many as you can?

While each of us has qualities characteristic of both psychocentrics and allocentrics, as well as a few of these specific types, we tend to fall somewhere along a continuum between extremes. The predictable psychocentrics would choose a place like Disney World for a preferred destination; allocentrics would choose instead a remote island in the South Pacific. Someone who is "mid-centric," or about halfway between the two extremes, might go to Europe or the Caribbean. Much depends, however, not only on where you go, but how you go. Here's how the types break out:

	PSYCHOCENTRIC	ALLOCENTRIC
Major Characteristics	Steady, passive, reflective	Gregarious, curious, adventurous
Preferred Destinations	Aspen, Disney World, Las Vegas, Club Med	Borneo, Tasmania, Sierra Club backpack
Mode of Travel	Car, tour bus, cruise ship	Plane, bicycle, walking

	PSYCHOCENTRIC	ALLOCENTRIC
Preferred Goals	Relaxation, mild simulation, trophies,	Activation, dramatic stimulation, growth
Learning Structures	Museums, tour guides, tour books	Homestays, impromptu conversations, novels

The travel industry, always interested in ways to market its products more effectively, has completed a number of other studies that classify prospective consumers according to their traits. One typology looks at the "peace and quiet" traveler whose ideal vacation would be a summer spent in a cabin by a remote lake, versus the "overseas" traveler who would like to see the world.

A more extensive study described by tourism researchers Edward Mayo and Lance Jarvis adds to the picture with other classifications. The "historical traveler" is driven to understand the past and sees vacations primarily as educational opportunities, especially for the benefit of children. Such a family would not only visit Disney World but also Epcot and Cape Canaveral. They frequent historical sites, battlefields, and museums.

The "recreational vehicle traveler" is like a turtle, with a home on its back. Such individuals tend to be more homebodies who like their things with them at all times. They tend to be older, more conservative, and more frugal than other groups. They have more time to look around, like the outdoors, and are leisure oriented.

The "pay later traveler" is credit oriented, feels no compunction about enjoying life now, paying for it later. They are the greatest risk takers in the bunch. They are more prone to adventure-based activities. They tend toward optimism and the other qualities of allocentrics or overseas travelers mentioned earlier.

Rating Your Own Preferences

While this research has been undertaken primarily so that tourist destinations can appeal more directly to their ideal customers' fantasies, we can also use the results to understand better our own urges to travel. You might consider your own preferences according to the scales shown in the Travel Dimension Scales.

You can use these scales to identify your own inclinations toward a particular kind of travel. Items 3, 4, 5, 6, and 9 are typical of conventional traveling. If you scored 20 or greater on these five scales, you

Travel Dimension Scales.

What's important to you during travel?	Not Important				Very Important
1. Exotic locales	1———2———3———4———5				
2. Opportunities for adventure	1———2———3———4———5				
3. Comfort and convenience	1———2———3———4———5				
4. Luxury	1———2———3———4———5				
5. Shopping and souvenirs	1———2———3———4———5				
6. Peace and quiet	1———2———3———4———5				
7. Interactions with local people	1———2———3———4———5				
8. Educational opportunities	1———2———3———4———5				
9. Get exactly what you pay for	1———2———3———4———5				
10. Flexible structure	1———2———3———4———5				

are a person who enjoys comfort far more than adventure potential. Since it is not natural for you to take risks and you don't ordinarily think of travel as an opportunity for growth, you will find it especially challenging to get outside your comfort zone and produce significant changes in your life.

Items 1, 2, 7, 8, and 10 are most critical for transformative travel. If you scored above 20 on these scales, then it is likely that you have already experienced a number of personal changes as a result of your travels. You tend to be a risk taker and enjoy seeking out new opportunities, as well as venturing into the unknown. Furthermore, when you travel, you are inclined to devote as much time and energy to meeting people as to seeing sights. You also understand well the benefits of being flexible and spontaneous in your decisions so that you can capitalize on opportunities as they arise.

It isn't necessary to identify with one of these extreme categories to get more out of your travel experiences. Among the kinds of trips that most people prefer to take, one recent study found that 25 percent of those surveyed would choose an active vacation such as rafting, hiking, or skiing. Another 25 percent would prefer a cultural and educational journey that included museums and historical sites. The majority of people, however, would just as soon relax at the beach or spa. Most people, in fact, see vacations not as the means to go to something new but as a way to escape, temporarily, from the stresses of their normal lives. Sometimes this can be taken to an extreme in which trips and their associated activities allow the traveler to avoid a real engagement with life.

Some Lousy Reasons to Travel

Nigel considers himself to be a fearless traveler and adventurer. He is a triathlete by lifestyle, scheduling at least two workouts of several hours daily to maintain the degree of fitness he requires for his races around the world. He rises before dawn each day, swims or runs or bikes for a few hours before work. His lunch break often involves a light workout, perhaps stretching or walking. He ends each day, as well, with one of several workouts on his schedule.

Nigel is training now for the Cradle Mountain race in Tasmania, a grueling fifty-mile trek across some of the most rugged terrain on Earth. He is focused completely on his goal of completing the race with a respectable time. As you might imagine, such single-minded devotion to this task means other things get sacrificed along the way— in Nigel's case, his marriage, his relationship with his children, and any opportunity for promotion at work.

Nigel may be fearless in the wilderness or on the road with fifty miles ahead of him, but he is frightened terribly by the prospect of real intimacy in relationships. He uses his traveling as a way to protect himself from getting hurt. He regulates his life so that there is just no time to become involved with anyone seriously. Even the friends he trains with, or the people he sees repeatedly at races around the world, studiously avoid much intimate contact. They talk a lot about their diets and training regimens but rarely about their feelings.

My point here is that travel can be taken to an extreme. Some people are inclined to use travel to evade responsibilities or distract themselves from aspects of their lives they would rather not face. It was Ralph Waldo Emerson who observed that people "run away to other countries because they are not good in their own, and run back to their own because they pass for nothing in new places." There is some merit to this idea that travel sometimes represents an escape from intimacy, from commitment, from responsibility. Emerson asks: "Who are you that have no task to keep you at home?"

While it takes courage to venture into unknown territory and wild places, it also requires a kind of fortitude to stick things out where you are. Some people use travel as a way to avoid dealing with important issues in their lives, as a means to put distance between themselves and others they find threatening. For those afraid of commitment or intimacy in relationships, taking a trip is just the solution. For those who are unable or unwilling to sink in roots to establish themselves, travel allows them an excuse to remain in motion. For others who do not have the patience and resolve to create a stable home life, a satisfying career, a web of lifelong friendships, travel permits them to keep running away.

We glorify those who are discoverers rather than those who remain home, whose labor makes such expeditions possible. We see courage only in what people do to cross mountains, not in what it takes to tend the fires back home.

The spiritual traveler, according to writer Gully Wells, is an intellectual road warrior, motivated primarily by curiosity and a hunger for adventure. These people live in anticipation of their next journey. "Unencumbered by a surplus of cash, and therefore uncorrupted by the siren song of material comfort, this type of travel addict prefers to lead with the mind."

Addict indeed. The travelholic is someone who must plan for the next trip even before the present one is completed. Wells warns that remaining in motion can become an escape from reality, a substitute for life. Although many individuals claim that regular trips help clear their minds, they also distract them from themselves. One woman, interviewed by Wells for his investigation on travel addiction, admitted that she stays on the road constantly as a photographer. She becomes anxious when she stays put for very long. "When I am not traveling, I am not so sure that I am alive."

She has lived in the same apartment for fifteen years but has never furnished it with anything more than a futon, a cappuccino machine, and a collection of stones from around the world. She has no long-term relationships and has no idea where the nearest supermarket or dry cleaner is to her home.

This woman travels not to change but to escape herself. She remains too busy to deal with any ongoing issues in her life except how to get from where she is now to where she has to be next.

Is this a bad thing for her? Not necessarily. There are far worse addictions for those who don't wish to face themselves. Under these circumstances, however, travel is not so much a way to stimulate real changes as to prevent them. This can be symptomatic of a number of problems.

- *Avoidance of intimacy.* It is very difficult to have a deep, committed relationship with anyone when you are rarely in one place. Just think about the image of a sailor with a lover at every port.
- *Reckless sensation seeking.* Some people whose normal lives feel empty and unfulfilling, who are addicted to the rush of risky endeavors, will put themselves in jeopardy to remind themselves they are alive.
- *Irresponsible binging.* Just as people run up their debts and credit cards on shopping sprees as an antidote for depression, people can travel for a similar purpose. For example, a young man spent a whole year paying for a trip that lasted a week, and was far more expensive than he could afford. This made him so depressed he took another trip to make himself feel better.
- *Distraction from core issues.* When the going gets tough, the tough stay put. A change of scenery works so well because you don't have to think about things you would rather avoid. Unfortunately, when you return, you are faced with the same problems you have been struggling with most of your life.
- *Acting out.* Just as teenagers will "act out" to show authority figures that they can't be controlled, adults as well will do things that are irresponsible just to prove they won't have their freedom restricted. Travel can be a way to punish others, to destroy a relationship on your own terms, to assert your independence, or perhaps even to express rage.
- *Control pain.* Most everyone has their favorite ways of soothing themselves during times of upheaval. Drugs and alcohol work quite well. Sometimes people prefer other addictions like compulsive exercise or overdevotion to work. Travel is another possibility that sometimes helps a person forget things that are painful, to medicate temporarily any uncomfortable symptoms.
- *Enable continued dysfunction.* The decision to take a trip, and its accompanying actions, affects not only the traveler but also everyone else in the family, whether they go along or not. Sometimes people are designated, unconsciously, to leave the scene as a way to protect the family from getting too close to things that might jeopardize the uneasy alliance. A father, for example, is trying to get closer to his son, a realignment in their relationship that feels threatening to the mother and other siblings. The kid is sent away to camp for the summer, thereby breaking up any possibility of reconciliation that would be uncomfortable for other family members to deal with.

- *Malingering.* Some people are just plain lazy. Period. They don't like to work. They just want to have fun. Travel is fun. So as long as you are away traveling you don't have to answer questions as to why you aren't doing anything else productive with your life. Travel seems like work, or at the very least, it keeps you in continuous movement so you can't be pinned down.

- *Isolation.* Finally, certain kinds of travel, like that of the hermit or solo adventurer, prevent any kind of deep relationships. While it is true you will get to know yourself under conditions of solitude, it may be at the expense of connecting to others in loving relationships.

There may be elements of several of these for any trip that you take. This is not necessarily a bad or an unhealthy situation; it depends on what exactly you are avoiding or hiding from. So consider your motivation for travel to determine if it might not be more transformative for you to stay home.

—∿—

I am proposing here a kind of journey, for the veteran as well as the neophyte, that doesn't so much help you recover from what you deal with on a daily basis as change how you look at your life and make decisions in the future. This type of profound change is possible only when you begin the process with adequate planning, not only regarding where you will go but how you will approach the entire experience.

4

Planning Your Trip

After you have clarified your own motivations and goals for your trip, the next stage involves constructing a flexible plan, one that gives you a rough guide for how you might meet your personal objectives. It is also crucial, however, that you remain willing to abandon your agenda and take advantage of any unexpected opportunity that comes along.

PREPARING YOURSELF MENTALLY

Most people limit their trip preparations to the basics of planning an itinerary and what they will carry in their luggage. Transformative travel, however, takes place on a level that is as much inside your head as it is in the outside world. If your goal is to promote personal change and growth, then you must take the same deliberate care in preparing yourself mentally as you do in packing your suitcases.

At the very least, you will wish to consider several questions that you can answer to your own satisfaction. Just before leaving for a week-long business trip, Marcia decided to build into the structure some opportunities for personal growth that she would not ordinarily have at home. Since her work would take up only a fraction of her time, she figured there were a number of ways she could act productively with a few of the morning, evening, and weekend hours that had been set aside for personal use.

Marcia got a late start with her mental planning, since the idea to make this business trip into a personally rewarding experience didn't crystallize until just before she boarded the plane. Nevertheless, she flipped open her laptop computer and wrote out brief responses to each of the following questions, which helped her focus on exactly what she wanted to accomplish and how she intended to reach her goals.

•   What is it that you would like to have happen as a result of your trip? *I wish I could feel less guilty and less burdened by my family, especially my two children, whom I feel like I'm neglecting because I am pursuing a career so ambitiously.*

•   In what specific ways would you like to be a different person from the one who left? *I know in this short period of time I can't completely rid myself of all guilt and uneasiness I feel related to balancing being a mother, wife, and professional, but I sure would like to dump a lot of these negative feelings.*

•   What has worked for you before during times when you have been interested in promoting personal changes? *Well, the last time I tried to do something like this, things didn't work out that well. That's because I didn't have a clear idea of what I wanted to accomplish. Once, though, I found it very helpful to break up my routines—not to spend time with the same people I usually do, not to order the same things I usually eat. If my goal is to come back different, then I need to experiment with new ways of being myself. It has also helped me a lot in the past when I rehearse in my head what might happen to throw me off course, so that I can plan how to counteract this.*

•   What can you do to set the stage before you leave that will give you a head start on your change efforts? *As soon as I'm done with these questions, I'm going to use this airphone to call my husband at the office and tell him what I'm up to and what I intend to work on while I'm gone. Even though he may not understand what I'm up to, initially, or even resist the idea since it will mean I am less manipulated by his attempts to have more of my attention, I'm confident he will come around. Even if he doesn't, this is something I have to do for myself or I will be no good for anyone else.*

- What do you need to take with you that will act as a support during times of difficulty? *I think what I need to do is some reading about guilt and how other women struggle with their dual roles. The first thing I'm going to do after I check in is find a bookstore. Then I need to think about who handles things pretty well among those I'll be spending time with during this trip. I can get support and encouragement from them when I feel myself slipping back to old habits. Also, I can call my sister a few times while I'm here. She has been the one all along who has been encouraging me to make some changes in my attitude.*

- How do you intend to structure your days so that they are more likely to produce the outcomes you are looking for? *There are several different things I can, no, I will do every day during this trip. First of all, I intend to spend some time each day talking to at least one professional woman, either an associate or a stranger I meet, about how she deals with her own feelings of ambition in light of her family. Secondly, when I call home each night—Wait a minute! That's another change I can make. I will not call home every night. When my husband goes out of town he expects me to handle things, so why shouldn't the reverse be true? Okay, I will only call home five out of the seven nights I am gone. Also, when I call home, I will not allow my husband to make me feel guilty about abandoning him. I won't even let him joke about it. Third, I'm going to do something nice for myself each day I'm gone—a massage one day, a special dinner, a new pair of shoes. Usually I spend all my time shopping for my husband and kids to appease my guilt.*

- What is it about the trip you are planning that you dread the most? *That's a no-brainer. When I do call home and my children say "Mommy, I miss you so much. When are you coming home?" Then the tears will flow. My husband will get on the phone next and pretend to kid me about traumatizing our kids. That's why I don't want to call home.*

- How will you motivate yourself to face that which you are avoiding? *I've got to try and handle things differently. I don't think it really matters much what I say to them on the phone. They won't understand anyway, since I haven't explained to them yet that I'm going to be making some changes. One thing I can do, though, is pretend this is a game. Their behavior is so predictable. I know exactly what will happen. In fact, I'm going to write out the script ahead of time so I don't let things get to me so much. The fact is that I do miss them too. I miss them already. Well, kind of.*

- How will you handle yourself when things don't go as expected? *I suppose because this is new territory for me it's expected that things won't go according to plan. I may even fall apart after I call them tonight. No, that's right. I'm not going to even call tonight. Well then, tomorrow when I call. I have to be forgiving of myself, to realize that even though I may have a few setbacks I am still going to do what I need to do. This is going to be difficult. That's why I need to get out of town in order to do it.*

• How do you intend to measure the effects of what you are attempting so you can demonstrate the success of your efforts? *Now I spend about a third of my time when I'm not otherwise occupied worrying about how I'm neglecting either my family or my job. If I could reduce that negative thinking to a fraction of that, say by 50 percent, that would be a great start. Eventually, I want to get to the point so I'm more like my husband in this regard. He doesn't feel like he is a terrible parent when he goes away or stays late at the office.*

• How will you follow through on what you started after you return home? *Yeah, that's the big question. I can do anything I want while I'm away. The true test is what happens when I get back. I think all throughout the rest of this week, I'm going to make a series of resolutions, write them down here, and follow them after I get home. The very first one is that I will have a very long talk with my husband to explain my position and solicit his support for what I intend to do. Next, I need to talk to my supervisor about things that she can do to help me make some changes at work as well.*

At about the time Marcia finished these words, she was warned that they were on their final approach for landing. As she returned her seat back to an upright position, fastened her seat belt, and returned her tray table to its original position, she nodded her head once, twice in resolve. In one week, she was determined to be a new person.

You may well have other questions you want to attend to, but these questions provide a good place to start. The chart on the following page provides a list for ready reference. Try keeping a copy in your desk or briefcase, and see where it takes you.

Modifying Expectations

Although preparation is important in structuring a transformative experience, there is a point at which you must let go of all your expectations and plans so you can grab onto opportunities as they arise spontaneously. It is too much structure rather than too much freedom that makes a journey all but worthless. You might as well stay home to see the movie.

Questions to Build Your Plan.

What is it that you would like to have happen as a result of your trip?

In what specific ways would you like to be a different person from the one who left?

What has worked for you before during times when you have been interested in promoting personal changes?

What can you do to set the stage before you leave that will give you a head start on your change efforts?

What do you need to take with you that will act as a support during times of difficulty?

How do you intend to structure your days so that they are more likely to produce the outcomes you are looking for?

What is it about the trip you are planning that you dread the most?

How will you motivate yourself to face that which you are avoiding?

How will you handle yourself when things don't go as expected?

How do you intend to measure the effects of what you are attempting so you can demonstrate the success of your efforts?

How will you follow through on what you started after you return home?

What is a bad trip, after all, Edward Hoagland wonders. Is it really when things go wrong? Just as often, it is when things go too right. From his own experience as a professional traveler, Hoagland concludes, "A bad trip is likely to be an organized trip with officious organizers, not a trip where reality intrudes its snaky head. I like both snakes and reality."

In spite of your best preparations, there is a point in every journey when you must discard your maps and guidebooks, ignore warnings of caution, and go forth bravely into the vast unknown. "All growth is a leap in the dark," Henry Miller once observed, "a spontaneous unpremeditated act without benefit of experience."

One of the most difficult tasks to complete prior to beginning a voyage is to let go of your expectations, to put aside your plans. That way you will rarely be disappointed.

In Anne Tyler's novel, *The Accidental Tourist,* the main character writes guidebooks for business travelers who would like to pretend they never left home. After his child is killed and his wife leaves him, his sense of compulsiveness, orderliness, and need for control become even more pronounced. Yet it is not through meticulous planning but through the serendipitous meeting with his dog's trainer that the wounded man heals himself. He learns that growth comes from accidental rather than deliberate encounters, that although people of his "traveling class" prefer controlling every facet of their journeys, it is only when you give up control to go with the flow that truly marvelous things can happen.

It is far better to empty yourself, to expect nothing and be pleasantly surprised by anything delightful that you encounter. Do your homework. Plan a rough itinerary if you must. Then let go of all your demands that things be a particular way for you to be satisfied. Erma Bombeck remarked on the phenomenon of how often her expectations limited her experiences: "Many times before travelers go to a country, they pack too much baggage—not necessarily clothes, but impressions of what the people are going to be like and how they will fit the stereotype fashioned for them."

After spending most of her life as a student of travel, writing fiction, memoirs, and guides about her adventures, Mary Morris concludes that all her most memorable experiences were unplanned and her most interesting encounters were accidental. It was when a train made an unscheduled stop, a bus never showed up, a policeman pulled her over for speeding, that real adventures occurred. Morris may not recall a single Hilton Hotel she's ever stayed in—but she remembers falling out of bed in Russia, sleeping in a box in Panajachel, or on a straw mat in Honduras.

It is not that travel must be uncomfortable or primitive or disastrous, just that it must remind you to be more alive. As Morris relates: "It is because of the unexpected that interesting things happen to us. And also because we allow them to happen."

Interesting wording: interesting things happen to those who allow them to happen.

Transformative travel begins to take place once you let go of your own schedule and pace, following the rhythms of the people and land you are visiting. Being "on time" is meaningless in this world of movement where the point, after all, is not to arrive somewhere but to get the most from the journey. Writing several decades ago about the quality of travel, British author Sybille Bedford said that the experience is essentially an engagement between ego and the world, a relationship that is, by its very nature, unpredictable: "The world is hydra-headed, as old as the rocks and as changing as the sea, enmeshed inextricably in its ways. The ego wants to arrive at places safely and on time."

There is an aspect of travel that involves giving up control. You find yourself in situations in which others hold your life in their hands. They make decisions that you must live with.

Take flying, for example. You are stuck in a metal cylinder hurtling through space. You can read or listen to music or talk to your seatmate, even eat a meal, but you can't get off when you want to. You put your faith in the competence of others—and you hope they know what they are doing.

Sometimes the others you put your faith in are not even human. As one man, now in his fifties, relates:

> I have done a lot of dangerous, adventurous things in my life, but by far the most terrifying thing I have ever done is ride a horse to a campsite in the Sierra Mountains. I have been rock climbing before. I have driven on roads in rural Mexico. I have scuba dived in some very precarious situations. Nothing, however, even came close to the fear of being at the mercy of these horses that kept struggling to maintain their balance on slippery rock. There was nothing I could do but hang on and try not to look at the thousand foot drop-offs on each side.

There is a liberation and freedom to giving up control as well. Since there is nothing you can do but hang on, there is no sense in worrying about what will happen. You may as well enjoy the ride as best you can. There is also something to be learned from the experience of letting go of control, as the man continues:

> I am someone who is used to being in control of every facet of my life. I plan every part of my day. Nothing is a surprise. Likewise, anything that happens, or doesn't happen, is the result of my efforts. I am used to not having anyone to blame when things go wrong. I like being responsible for how things go. But here was a situation in which I had no control. I wasn't even steering the damn horse! As terrified as I was, on some level I did enjoy depending on someone else for a change.

CHOOSING A TRANSFORMATIVE PATH

It is time to plan your next trip. You have decided that you want something more than a vacation, a mere respite in your otherwise chaotic life. You want to come back recharged, if not reborn. So what do you do? Call your travel agent and say you want a life-changing trip? If only it was that easy.

There are several strategies that are part of meaningful travels, several internal attitudes that can help you change yourself dramatically in a remarkably short period of time. For example, it is a good idea to have some idea of what kind of change you are looking for so you can plan an experience that is most likely to produce desirable results. Is it solitude you are after, or rather more enriched relationships with others? Is your primary problem that you have too much going on in your life, or not enough stimulation? Is a structured trip going to serve you best, or perhaps one in which you follow your daily whims? What outcome would you like to happen ideally as a result of this journey? Once you have answered these questions, you can more easily target a particular kind of trip, or at least limit your investigations to specific areas.

Progressing Through Stages

Read books. Talk to people. Interview others who have been transformed by their travels. Find out where they went, what they did, and what they experienced. Most of all, pay attention to what has worked for you before, what hasn't had much enduring impact, and where you are right now in your stages of travel.

Melanie has traveled her whole life. Her office and home are filled with artifacts from her various journeys. Tapestries from Bolivia, Costa Rica, and Turkey adorn her walls. Statues, knickknacks, wood carvings, religious icons, baskets are displayed from five continents.

Usually never at a loss for words, nor hesitant about telling her adventures, Melanie was uncharacteristically pensive about one question I asked her. Once, twice, she was about to answer, then checked herself, unsatisfied with the prepared response. Finally, she just looked at me apologetically and shrugged. "It all depends on where I was in my life. It took something different when I was younger than it would take now."

The question I asked Melanie, if you haven't already guessed, was what she found most stimulating about travel. During her teens, just the idea of being away from home was utterly amazing. She could stay up as late as she wanted and be friends with whomever she liked. During her twenties, romance was most important. She also hungered for physical challenges—climbing peaks, walking long distances, bicycling cross country. This, she claimed, gave her confidence to conquer other goals at work.

In her thirties, she felt most changed by spiritual encounters. She spent a lot of time visiting churches and religious sites of special significance. Now in her forties, Melanie believes that it takes a lot more, and yet a lot less, to move her. She has seen it all, done it all. Twice. It is simple things now that have the most impact—the colors of a sunset she has never seen in that way before, the shy smile of a begging child that continues to haunt her, the smell of an open sewer, or the kindness of a stranger who rescued her from a sticky situation.

Melanie no longer buys things when she travels, nor does she bother to take photographs. "I'm beyond that point where I want to collect anything," she explains. Her progression illustrates the stages of the traveler, how change occurs by different means depending on your level of experience and what is going on in your life at the time.

Choosing Places to Stay

The choice about where to stay should be related to what kind of trip will promote the personal changes you desire. While staying in a hotel or resort might be the logical, convenient alternative for some people, such facilities also have the disadvantage of insulating you more from the local culture and people.

While staying in a bed and breakfast gives you some taste for local customs, arranging a homestay in which you live with a local family is even better. During a recent visit to Australia, I had arranged through electronic mail a number of contacts with colleagues in various places I would be visiting. What made my trip so transformative was staying in people's homes along the way. Ordinarily, my privacy is very important to me. I actually *like* the antiseptic, impersonal quality of hotels that make me feel anonymous. I figured, however, that the trip would be far more interesting for me if I attempted to do that which I found most uncomfortable.

To my surprise, I discovered that the best part of my journey was joining the families of various Australians. I became part of the extended family of a retired couple, then a pair of young newlyweds, then the chaotic home of a family with nine children. In each case, I met their friends, followed them around, lived their lives not only as a guest but a welcome member of their tribe. More than any other experience, creating the opportunity to live alternative lifestyles helps you examine your own choices.

Homestays are arranged for visiting students and scholars in which they pay a weekly fee to live with a local family, not as a stranger but a welcome member. This is exactly the experience that Peace Corps volunteers report was so meaningful to them, even when they didn't particularly care for the people with whom they lived.

Short of joining the Peace Corps, or the army, or taking a year off as an exchange student, how do you arrange such a placement? It's actually easier than you might imagine. If, for example, a friend, or a friend of a friend, told you that a visitor from Japan or Turkey or Indonesia was going to be in town for a week or so, and rather than staying in a hotel, she preferred to say with an American family, wouldn't you consider the opportunity? Perhaps you don't have the room, or your family wouldn't adapt well to a stranger in their midst, or the idea doesn't sound very appealing, but I can promise you that it surely does seem interesting to many people around the world.

Finding Educational Opportunities

Organizations such as the Council on International Education Exchange arrange extended travel opportunities for students to study or work abroad. They also set up learning vacations for professionals, teachers, and seniors who are interested in making their vacations into something more than a pleasant diversion.

Homestays and home exchanges can also be arranged through various groups, many of which are described in guidebooks published by the Council. (The Further Reading section lists one such resource, edited by Priscilla Tovey.) For the mature traveler, as well, organizations such as the American Association of Retired Persons, Mature Outlook, and Elderhostel plan trips that are designed to educate as well as to entertain.

Literally thousands of tour groups, universities, and nonprofit agencies organize archaeological and anthropological expeditions, architectural and urban planning tours, art appreciation programs, intensive language training abroad, nature and science trips, outdoor adventures, theological and religious pilgrimages, and community service projects. While the intent of these programs is primarily to stimulate the mind, even structured education can be transformative on multiple levels of moral, emotional, spiritual, and intellectual development when it takes place in another culture. This is especially the case when you make an effort to break away from the security of the structured program to venture out on your own.

Organized Destinations

Some people don't want to leave things to chance. If you are going to devote time, energy, and money to producing some sort of therapeutic change, you may not want to just wander around somewhere, staying in people's homes, walking whenever you can, and hoping for the best. The good news is that there are a number of outfits that specialize in providing personal change opportunities for travelers. Most have a new-age bent to them, designed for people who are looking for growth in a number of realms. The possibilities are staggering, if not endless.

In one international directory that lists retreats and adventures for the growth minded, John Benson organizes the options available. There are 200 different places you can go for meditation training, including guided visualization, nature and device attunement, and of course, interspecies communication. This doesn't include another 150 options for hatha yoga. Then there are categories of movement (aikido, tai chi), psychic healing (aura cleansing, chakra balancing), power places (earth vortexes, religious apparitions), vision quests (solo wilderness vigils with or without fasting), and bodywork (shiatsu, Rolfing). For those who are somewhat more conventionally minded, there are also quite a number of retreat centers, self-expression programs, spas, and counseling centers that are all geared toward helping people make changes in their body image or self-concept away from home.

You could, for example, spend time at a Tibetan monastery or an Arizona health spa, take a tour with a clairvoyant in Nepal, go on a vision quest on an Indian reservation or a woman's spirituality retreat, or visit a dude ranch in Montana. All these places cater to different tastes, yet with a similar goal—to provide an environment the leaders believe is most conducive to personal change. Since each of us is at a different stage in life, has unique interests and values, and is struggling with different issues, it makes sense that a number of varied environments might conceivably produce similar personal gains. The difficult challenge is finding or creating the place that might work best for you.

Regardless of where you go, and whether you join a structured program or venture off on your own, you will want to make sure that the following elements are in evidence:

- There are tests and challenges that will push you to discover new capabilities.
- There is support available should you find yourself in immediate physical or psychological danger.
- There are situations that allow you to experiment with alternative roles and ways of being.

- There are forced opportunities to interact with people in intimate ways.
- There is a balance between time with yourself and time with others.
- There is a commitment not only to look outward at new, exotic scenes, but also to look inward at how everything is affecting you.
- There are situations that engage not only your body and mind, but also heart and soul.
- There are experiences that shake your core, that turn your world upside down in such a way that things will never look the same again.
- There are opportunities to reflect on and process your experiences constructively, to create meaning from what you have lived.
- There are ways that you can apply what you learned to your life back home and actually follow through with your intentions.
- There are ongoing ways in which you can monitor your continued progress and be accountable to yourself for reaching desired goals.
- There are ways that you can integrate personal growth within the context of your most significant relationships back home.

THE QUESTION OF COMPANIONSHIP

The issue of relationships brings to focus the very important decision about whether the best trip for you might be in the accompany of others, whether family or a tour group, or as a solitary adventure. Although many people don't often choose to travel alone when potential companions are available, there are a number of advantages to doing so.

Traveling Solo

The solitary traveler has been romanticized by so many writers. In its purest form, Jonathan Raban muses, travel "requires no certain destination, no fixed itinerary, no reservations, and no return ticket, for you are trying to launch yourself onto the haphazard drift of things and put yourself in the way of whatever chances the journey throws up." Loneliness, he writes further, is an essential ingredient for good traveling; it pushes you to take risks you would never dare at home. "It's when you haven't spoken to a soul for days, when your whole being feels possessed by the rage for company, that even the withdrawn social coward feels an invigorating rush of desperate courage."

In spite of this inspirational advice, traveling alone is no easy matter, especially when feelings of loneliness and isolation set in. When things really start to feel weird, when you sense panic creeping in, it is time for the "traveler's meditation" Carl Franz describes in his guidebook to Mexico. First, you find a nice room to spend the night, perhaps one that is even a little beyond your usual budget. Second, you don't worry about the price.

You go to your room and strip off all your clothes. You take a hot shower or bath and then lie down for at least an hour. Breathe deeply. Think about gentle waves, clouds floating, or something else relaxing. Breathe deeply.

"When you're ready to face the world again, get up, put on your clothes and stroll calmly out of the room. The secret is to move and think *slowly,* to respond to people and events with the same serene, deliberate manner that you do at home. . . .

"Now glide on down the street, absorbing the scenery. Cross at proper intersections to avoid nerve shattering near misses. Find a pleasant cafe or park bench. Sit down. Let it all flow around you."

This is good advice for the solo traveler. It is not uncommon that you will feel weird and out of sorts when you are traveling alone, even if you ordinarily live by yourself. For those who travel alone but prefer to eat dinner in the company of others, Jennifer Cecil has compiled a whole volume of options. There are special cruise ships, spas, cooking or language schools, rafting or hiking trips, tennis or dude ranches, nature or photographic safaris, skiing or scuba trips, that all cater to the solo traveler, especially those who want limited companionship. The point here is that there are no excuses for avoiding a transformative trip just because you can't find someone to go with you. In many ways, the growth you will experience will be several times what it would have been if you had brought familiar faces with you.

Changing Relationships Forever

Beth Livermore, on safari in Africa, found herself trapped in a Land Rover between a raging elephant on one side and a lake filled with notoriously unpredictable hippopotamuses on the other side. On the edge of panic, she gripped the steering wheel and turned to her companion, who happened to be her mother. Her mother smiled reassuringly and said, "One day this will make a funny story."

At that moment, Beth realized how close she had grown to her mother during their brief week in Tanzania. Although the trip initially seemed to be about observing wildlife, photographing sunsets, and experiencing the Serengeti in all its splendor, its most enduring and meaningful effects were what it did for their relationship.

On their last evening together, they checked off a list of the trip's highlights—watching cheetahs in full flight, wildebeests grazing, sunrises and sunsets over the African plains. It was a charmed journey, they both agreed: "For besides having fun, we reclaimed the common ground that had been eroded by time and separation. And I was reminded of my mother's role as mentor. She helped cultivate my love of adventure. She gave me heart. She gave me soul. And nowhere could this have been made more apparent than in the mysterious land of Africa."

Travel does change relationships forever, for better or worse. Either the inevitable annoyances, discomforts, and stress get to you and you take out the frustration on your companions, or it makes you closer, bonded together by your shared experiences. There is indeed a special love and respect that develops among travelers, just as among soldiers, who must face adversity together as well as share magical moments. That is why marriages begin with a honeymoon, a special trip away from normal life that gives the couple time to bond, as well as create new experiences.

Think of the times you have had your most meaningful experiences on trips. There were times when you were alone, and actually being alone is what made them special. Yet it is so difficult to describe exactly what happened and how you felt to others who weren't there, much less explain it.

Then there are the incidents that were shared with someone else, whether a friend, lover, family member, or business associate. It is now a communal experience, one that grows each time stories are relived and reminiscences described to others.

Certainly there is growth possible when you are alone that just can't be touched when you have others to depend on. But it's a different kind of transformation altogether that bonds you closer to others as a result of what you've lived together. Intimacy and trust build so much quicker during travels. Years of steady growth can be compressed into a matter of weeks, if not days, during the accelerated pace of a vacation when many rules are suspended.

One couple who had been married over twenty years decided to spend two weeks backpacking together in a wilderness area: "It was absolutely glorious. We slogged through muddy bogs, forged through rivers, tramped through forests, skipped along beaches. We dealt with snakes and mosquitoes and some creatures we never saw who kept raiding our food supply. Sometimes we were exhausted, frightened, or lost. Most of the time we were sore, hungry, or lost. Yet the closeness we felt together—I wouldn't trade that for anything."

What happened to this couple occurs even faster with lovers who meet for the first time. People are more likely to fall in love on cruise ships or Club Meds because they know from the outset that the functional life span is one week. There is no time to play games. People are also more inclined to grow closer together because they take time for each other in ways they rarely do at home.

Just as in group or family therapy, where change often occurs more quickly than in individual sessions, so too do the dynamics between people when traveling heighten transformative effects. During one of his trips, Mark Twain noted just this phenomenon when he said: "I have found that there ain't no surer way to find out whether you like people or hate them than to travel with them."

There are a number of therapeutic ingredients that operate among interconnected people who are engaged in a process of mutual searching. Relationships become intensified. People come together in mutual support during difficult times. Vicarious learning takes place in which you grow as a result of watching others taking risks. There is a cathartic process as people share themselves in intimate ways and talk about what they are experiencing. In addition, just as with one of the greatest benefits of group therapy, you will often hear honest feedback from companions about things they most appreciate about you, as well as things you might consider changing.

Like other therapeutic groups, travel companions develop a level of trust and closeness that is unrivaled. A father relates the moving story of his family's summer vacation:

For the first six hours we all piled into the cab of the camper we were all at each other's throats. The girls were fighting. My wife and I kept arguing about where to go or how to get there. Both of us bickered at our daughters, and they yelled back at us as well.

Then, as the hours went by, something miraculous happened. I don't think we ever felt so close as a family, nor will we ever again. It was so wonderful to be together in that way. We talked and talked. The girls told us things about themselves we never imagined. In this same spirit of openness, my wife and I confided in them as we never had before.

The trip changed us. It really did. Years from now we won't remember exactly where we went, somewhere in the Northwest, but each of us will always remember the closeness we felt to one another.

That summer also meant so much to me because it was the summer before our eldest daughter went away to college. It was the last time we will ever be together like that again. And it was the best time.

This is not an unusual tale in the archives of most families who can recall their own most memorable travels. For one of the few times in her public persona, humorist Erma Bombeck became achingly serious when talking about the role that travel played in her family, especially as transitions from one stage to another. During what she described as a summer of discontent Bombeck and her family took a rafting trip: "For the first time we could remember, we were a family who gave one another space to be ourselves. We had never done that before. It was as if we all knew that this was the end of a chapter in our lives and the beginning of a new one. The umbilical cord that had bound us together as a unit for nearly two decades was about to be severed."

It was this trip on the Colorado River that became the most crucial transition of their lives. During their week on the rapids together they learned to see one another for the first time as contemporaries: "It was the last summer of the child . . . the last summer of the parents."

MAKE YOUR LIST, CHECK IT TWICE, THEN THROW IT AWAY

Regardless of whether you travel alone, with your family, or with a group, whether you go as part of an organized group or on your own, whether your intent is to change a little or a lot, personal changes are far more likely when you remain open to opportunities that arise.

In the early years of the Peace Corps, when volunteers were trained for field experiences abroad, they were sent to traditional universities where they spent time reading voraciously about their host countries and studying the economic, political, and social conditions under which they would operate. Although this seemed to follow a logical plan, the training ended up being woefully insufficient for people dealing with very complex tasks in very ambiguous situations. They may have had a solid academic, intellectual preparation to carry out their assignments but they were often overwhelmed by circumstances outside their control.

Reflecting back on his experience as Peace Corps trainer during these early years, Richard Hopkins observed that what these traveling change agents needed most to survive on foreign soil, much less to flourish, was a distinct set of skills that are not learned from books but from direct experience. Specifically, the volunteers needed to learn how to deal with ambiguity gracefully. They needed to raise their frustration tolerance levels to the point where they could handle disappointments, setbacks, and unforeseen outcomes with flexibility and good humor. They had to become good at dealing with periods of isolation and loneliness. Most of all, they had to become experts at learning from their own mistakes.

Hopkins compares the difference, for example, between language learned by a student in classroom drills and language learned by a traveler with a phrase book. Nothing will teach you faster than having to find a bathroom in a country where you don't speak the language.

One reason why traveling teaches so much more, so much faster, is that there is an immediate, visceral connection between what you do and how you get your needs met. I am speaking here of very basic needs, too—finding food, maintaining your safety, transporting yourself from place to place, keeping yourself occupied along the way.

Just like the Peace Corps volunteers, every traveler lives in an environment that is strange and unpredictable. The single most critical skill in such a setting is adaptability. Can you change your strategy or behavior in light of circumstances that are not what they once were, nor even what they first appeared to be?

Since you can't anticipate with any degree of certainty what you will encounter during travels, the best you can do is to make yourself fluid and flexible, to change according to the circumstances. This means being open and willing to acknowledge when something you are doing isn't working and being prepared to try something else.

Miriam couldn't figure out why the waiter kept bringing out the wrong order. Her request, she believed, was quite simple. She wanted scrambled eggs and toast, no bacon. "*Sin carne,*" she emphasized carefully, although the item on the menu had said bacon and eggs.

When the waiter brought out eggs scrambled with bits of bacon, she explained a second time in slow Spanish, "*Por favor. No me gusta el carne. No quiero el carne. Entiende?*"

The waiter nodded, returning to the kitchen. A few minutes later he returned with her plate of eggs. This time the bacon had been picked out, sorted, and neatly piled on the corner of her plate. Miriam could see the congealed bacon grease puddles where her eggs were now residing.

She tried for a third time, explaining again to the waiter what she wanted. This time she made sure she was understood, asking him to repeat back the order. Satisfied, she released him, saying a prayer to herself. In Spanish yet.

When the eggs landed on her table, wrong again, she had enough. Miriam threw money on the table and stormed out of the restaurant convinced she was surrounded by idiots. What had happened, however, was a misunderstanding in which the restaurant staff were as convinced Miriam was insane as she was certain of their stupidity.

Her mistake was not in what she ordered, or even how she ordered it, but in refusing to acknowledge that what she was doing was not getting her what she wanted. Rather than giving up her first, preferred strategy (verbal orders in Spanish, using the same vocabulary) and try something else (different vocabulary, different language, different dish), she persisted in actions that were ineffective not once, but four times. Partially, this rigidity comes from arrogance, from the belief you are right and everyone else is wrong. It also stems from a failure to monitor your mistakes so that you can correct them.

—⁓—

The preparations that you make for an upcoming transformative trip should include far more than reading guidebooks and talking to people. Since most personal changes occur inside your own mind, it is there that you should also be preparing yourself to encounter new experiences with grace and good will. Go ahead and make your lists, check them twice, then throw them away and go with the flow of what unfolds before you.

5

Doing What Comes Unnaturally

*Y*ou understand the reasons that most people travel. You have some idea as to what you are searching for in your next vacation and even what motivates your journey. How do you begin the process of planning a trip in such a way that you are most likely to find what you are looking for?

As you probably already realize, major changes don't come about without a certain amount of discomfort and inconvenience. In a sense, it is unnatural to place yourself in circumstances that are going to force you to struggle a bit. This is exactly what you will plan for in a life-altering adventure.

HOW CHANGE HAPPENS

You sleep and eat differently when you are on the road. You wear different clothes. You talk to people in ways in which you sometimes don't recognize yourself; it's as if someone else is speaking from inside your body. You take time to notice things that usually escape your attention. You visit unusual places, experiment with new activities. Strangeness and novelty are pervasive. All this leads to the formation of original ideas you had never considered before. Your attitudes become more flexible, or at least more transparent as they clash with those of others around you.

Since what you would normally do often doesn't work very well in the places you're visiting, you are forced to invent new ways of getting things done. Regardless of the ways you conduct yourself, travel places you in an assortment of situations every day, sometimes every hour, in which you can't depend on your time-honored strategies.

It is natural when you are away from home to cling to those things that are most familiar. You may go to restaurants and stay in hotels that supply comfortable environments. But change comes only with taking risks—both physical and psychological risks. The object of truly transformative travel is to shake your core, to alter your identity, to push you beyond your present levels of thinking and reacting. This will only take place when you force yourself to do the things that feel most unnatural, at least those that you are fairly certain are constructive rather than reckless or self-destructive.

Looking for Novelty

Change is actually a fairly ugly business. It means chaos and disorientation. It is unnatural to subject yourself willingly to situations that are likely to make you feel uncomfortable, that force you to work hard. That is why people don't often go looking for transformative experiences; more likely, such experiences search us out when we least expect it. Real, dramatic, life-altering changes often come upon us when we are looking the other way.

In one well-controlled study of 154 exchange students who spent one-month homestays in Japan, Michael Stitsworth investigated personality changes that resulted from the sojourn. Although anecdotal studies derived from travelers' journals and self-reports have claimed that such cultural immersions produce dramatic changes, this was one of the first empirical studies designed to measure to what extent people changed, and specifically how they changed.

The results bore out the anecdotal findings, but with some interesting twists. For example, the students who experienced the most dramatic changes were those who had never been abroad before, nor had anyone else in their families. They weren't really looking for any type of personal changes. In fact, they didn't really know what to expect from the experience.

Second, those who had little exposure to foreign language training changed far more than those who had studied a second language for a year or more. Apparently, their relative naïveté regarding cultural differences, even the little bit that people are exposed to when learning another language, made them even more ripe for change. These individuals developed increased flexibility, independence, and creative thinking during their trip.

As noted in the previous chapter, the point isn't that you should minimize preparation in the planning of your own trip or that ignorance is better than being informed; rather, it is that novelty is what gets your attention and makes change possible. When you open yourself up to new experiences, holding expectations and preconceptions in check, you are more likely to be influenced by what you run into.

Planning for Spontaneity

In spite of your best planning and preparation, your most enthusiastic intentions to make an experience worthwhile, the ultimate outcome depends on factors outside your control. Whether sailing, surfing, or anything else, you can have the best possible equipment and training, be poised perfectly to ride the perfect wind or wave, but when things come together magically it is frequently because you were willing to make instantaneous adjustments that let you take advantage of the situation that presented itself.

You may think, for example, that the best part of your day is going to be attending a play you have been looking forward to. In fact, it may very well be the conversation you have with someone while standing in line for tickets that has the most enduring impact. Or perhaps it's not the play itself that becomes so stimulating as what a few of the images portrayed on stage spark within you. A whole act goes by while you are lost in your own thoughts, making connections between the present and the past, between what you saw and what you've lived before, and what you now intend to live in the future. You weren't looking for this change. It happened while you were enjoying yourself during an evening's entertainment.

This book is about making change happen rather than merely waiting for it to occur. There are limits, however, to what you can force, even with the highest possible motivation and determination. The best you can reasonably expect is to place yourself in the circumstances you've constructed that may lead to certain outcomes.

You can put yourself in the most spectacular setting, equip yourself with the best camera and the best film, find the ideal perch from which to capture the scene, yet if the light does not cooperate—if it is too harsh or too subdued—your efforts will be largely wasted. Even for professional photographers, the best photos tend to be the ones snapped during a moment's inspiration. That is exactly what happens with transformative travel as well: you have to be ready, at a second's notice, to jump on that perfect wave. There might not be another one coming for a long, long time.

TYPES OF CHANGE

The metaphor of comparing the change process to a big wave can be taken further, for both phenomena can be exhilarating or very destructive. In addition to their similar unpredictable nature, each demonstrates remarkable individuality in its form. For example, I speak of change as if it is a single process. Actually, it involves three distinctly different types.

Developmental Changes

Change is an integral, continual process that unfolds throughout your life span. It is not so much steady growth as it is periodic spurts of maturity. Critical transition points occur in the life of a traveler. At age sixteen months we deal with separation from parents manifested in symptoms of stranger anxiety; acute fear sets in when we realize we are on our own. Again at age three or four years, once we enter preschool, we are forced to confront the reality that we travel life alone. And so on from early childhood through later maturity, we confront a series of developmental tasks or transition points that must be negotiated successfully or we will forever remain "travel retarded," so to speak.

One dramatic example of such a critical incident is your earliest memory of being lost. Whether separated from your parents at a mall, lost in a new neighborhood, or accidentally isolated from a group during a school field trip, you will never forget that terrifying feeling of having no idea where you are, nor the slightest inkling of where to go next. Presumably there was a happy ending (because you are here to read this) even though you carry within you those first feelings of panic that still creep up whenever you are lost to this day. How you deal with the frustration and fear in the present is related to how well you handled similar challenges in the past.

As disconcerting as developmental crises may be, they are essentially predictable events. You may not like dealing with physical changes like puberty or menopause, family changes involving the care of an aging parent or rebellious teenager, or other emotional changes associated with different stages of life, but you aren't completely taken by surprise when they arrive. You can prepare for these developmental transitions just as you can anticipate comparable travel challenges along the road. It is a virtual certainty, for example, that at some point you will deal with delayed flights, lost baggage, rude staff, and yes, becoming lost yourself.

Situational Changes

Some changes may be imaginable but neither predictable nor anticipated. You might consider it entirely possible that you could be involved in a serious car, plane, or train wreck. You may even know someone who has had such a misfortune. But you would not expect that a situational disaster would befall you as surely as you will face developmental changes.

Argentine novelist Alberto Manguel describes the birth of his beliefs as a moderate anarchist, the result of a situational change in which he faced the pesky, prissy bureaucrats who are given the uniforms and power to squeeze people's toothpaste and decide who may enter their countries. Such run-ins with officious personnel are often the first encounters we have when we arrive at a new place, not to mention the last we see as our trip ends.

During such situations we learn about powerlessness. We are at the whims of inspectors who are, by nature, suspicious and haughty. They are looking for criminals, smugglers, illegal aliens, and a good thing too. But we are also caught in their webs, subject to delays at best, and possibly strip searches and other indignities as well.

Make no mistake, however, as much as we would like to forget these experiences, they indelibly stamp their distasteful images on our psyches. It's no wonder that such skirmishes lead to resentment if not revolution. Wars were started for less.

Discontinuous Change

Adult development specialist Judy-Arin Krupp describes this third type of transformation as being the most influential because the precipitating events can't even be imagined. You are so taken by surprise that any preparation for dealing with the stressful event is impossible. How, for example, could you ever ready yourself to deal with being robbed—or for that matter, with winning the lottery? Perhaps surprisingly, both these predicaments place people in situations that they rarely deal with effectively.

Krupp contends that people dread change so much primarily because they worry about trauma for which they will have little preparation or control. The solution, of course, is to equip yourself as best you can with whatever resources and skills you might need, regardless of the situation.

I worked for a while with a woman who was inclined toward acute anxiety, if not panic attacks, when faced with any novel situation. Traveling was out of the question. She wouldn't even drive through tunnels or over bridges because of the perceived restrictions on her freedom. To make matters worse, this woman was adamant about not ingesting any foreign substance like medicine into her body. Although this was a case in which antianxiety medication might have helped her, she refused to succumb to what she called "crutches" for aid during difficult times.

I applauded her resolve and courage to manage her fears on her own, especially in these times where almost everyone is looking for a pill to swallow their troubles away. The compromise we worked out is that she would carry in her purse a vial of the lowest dose possible of Xanax, a mild tranquilizer. She never actually needed to take a pill, even when she felt her control slipping. Just knowing she had the pills available, however, that she could take one if things got really bad, was enough of a safety net to permit her to try to deal with risks she would not otherwise have considered.

Through sufficient training and preparation, each of us can equip ourselves with "pills," metaphorically speaking, that we can rely on during times of need.

By definition, discontinuous changes occur when we must face new situations in which we have little prior experience. Everything we do under such circumstances is experimental, and probably quite awkward since we have had little practice. If we are learning something new, whether riding a bike for the first time, reading a magnetic compass, or navigating through an urban subway system, we are not going to be particularly graceful or accomplished in our efforts. Survival is the major objective; expecting anything more is unreasonable.

Interestingly, once you log experience surviving discontinuous changes, even growing as a result, you are able to generalize these skills to other crises that can occur in the future. You may have never before had to deal with the discomfort of spending two days in a grim hotel room puking your guts out as a result of something you ate, but you have faced other travel challenges just as serious. What you learned previously is that complaining and pouting don't work nearly as well as making the best of a situation and taking whatever precious moments of comfort you can find.

WHAT PRODUCES POSITIVE CHANGE?

In planning your own trip, you are not interested in all sorts of changes, just in those that are constructive in your life. Behaviors that might initially feel unnatural eventually become a part of your normal functioning when you have had sufficient practice. This is more likely to take place when you construct conditions that are most often associated with positive changes, whether in the context of psychotherapy, education, or travel.

Perception of Freedom

In an ideal classroom, in a therapy session, or in the best that travel has to offer, there are opportunities to experiment with alternative ways of being. You are able to break out of ruts that have kept you stuck in the same track. What travel offers is the opportunity to alter the patterns with which you live your life.

Examine the ways you feel constricted in your life. There are so many ways in which it feels like choices are made for you—what you will do, where, how, and with whom you will do it. Even your few precious hours of leisure each day are overstructured with obligations and responsibilities. This has become so familiar it almost feels natural.

Doing what comes unnaturally means planning a trip in which you will have unstructured blocks of time when you are not required to do anything in particular. Only under the circumstances of maximum freedom can you truly experiment with alternative ways of being.

Safe Risks

Freedom to try out new skills, behaviors, attitudes, and ways of functioning is hardly transformative unless you feel motivated to get outside your comfort zone. If you are going to experiment with alternative ways to make decisions, or handle yourself during particular moments, then you want to feel that making inevitable mistakes will not result in catastrophe.

You can deliberately plan opportunities to try new behaviors in measured doses. This means looking at things you are about to do that seem too easy and natural, asking yourself what you could do instead that might be more interesting, then pushing yourself to follow through on those tasks. For example, one man on a routine business trip was about to hail a taxi to the site of a scheduled appointment. He had time to kill. He was feeling in an adventurous mood. So instead he got directions to the closest bus stop and found out how he could negotiate across town using public transport. This may not sound like a big deal to you but it was downright miraculous in the context of his life.

The question for your own planning is: What can *you* do that would be a departure from your usual routines?

Teachable Moments

Why is it that someone can say something to you in one situation and the words go right through you, yet in quite another setting someone can tell you the exact same thing and it blows you away? There are particular teachable moments when you are unusually susceptible to being influenced by what you are experiencing. It is almost a hypnotic state in which you are hypersuggestible to whatever is being offered. This happens in therapy by design when the professional deliberately controls the circumstances so that what transpires has the maximum impact on the client. The same things can happen when you are traveling, if these other conditions are in evidence.

One man, for example, recalls his most impressionable travel experience as being completely unexpected:

> I was in Florence, Italy, seeing the sights. I stood before Michelangelo's "David," utterly stunned. I'd seen photos of it, of course, but I had no idea how powerfully moved I'd be by seeing it in person. All at once, I felt an appreciation for the male body that I'd never known before.

Part of it, I suppose, was disconcerting because I became aware of feeling incredibly attracted to the male form. Although I love women very much, I realized also the incredible beauty of a man's body. Somehow, seeing that perfect male form allowed me to appreciate better my own body, to see the attraction of other men without any longer feeling embarrassed.

These teachable moments can occur at any time, but so often they do take place during travels. Being in foreign territory strips away our defenses and ordinary ways of processing information. You are more vulnerable but also more open to what is going on around you, and within you.

Emotional Arousal

Change takes place when emotions are stirred up in such a way that your head, your heart, and your soul are all humming along. Intense emotion activates your nervous system in a way that makes you far more likely to remember what is happening. When you are feeling something intensely, *anything*—whether fear, elation, or apprehension—your brain is far more susceptible to being influenced by the experience.

Emotional activation is the logical outcome, if not the goal, of transformative travel. What you are trying to do is to stir yourself up in a way that will produce alternative ways of looking at things. In a sense, you are trying to elicit tears, not only of transcendence, appreciation, and joy, but also of frustration, anger, and sadness. It is intensity you are after, for during this state of vulnerability you are far more likely to become transformed, for better or worse.

In describing the process by which emotional, visceral experiences dramatically shape the future paths lives take, educator Stephen Brookfield relates an incident that took place while he was spending a few months abroad. Until that point in his life—the ripe age of forty—he had somehow managed to avoid learning to drive a car. Something about being in a novel environment encouraged him to take risks he would not have otherwise considered.

While staying in Italy, Brookfield took to the wheel for the first time. Giddy with his rapid progress after a lifetime of driving avoidance, he insisted one rainy evening that he be allowed to transport his family through the countryside. The task at hand was far more than he could handle, producing a few close calls before he was banished to the backseat: "I let my wife take the wheel and I sank into a near catatonic state, a state I imagine resembles the falsely comforting ener- vation travelers trapped in snow drifts feel just before they slip into their last sleep."

Discouraged by this episode, Brookfield reflected that while being away from home encouraged him in the misguided belief he could do most anything, he learned lessons about the dangers of getting car- ried away with visions of personal empowerment. Furthermore, it was the intensely emotional nature of this experience that made it so unforgettable. Significant learning is, by its very nature, an active process, one in which you are engaged not just with your brain but with your heart, not just with intellect but with deep feelings.

Problem Solving

Travel is really about solving problems. How will you get from one place to another? Where will you sleep and eat when you get there? How will you spend your time? How can you get the most entertain- ment for your investment? How can you get this merchant to sell you something for less money?

Transformative travel promotes a kind of problem solving that results in some enduring solutions, especially those that you might apply to other situations in your life. For example, you are confronted by a predicament in which the hotel you had booked a confirmed reservation refuses to acknowledge that you exist. You complain but are firmly rebuffed. You whine—to no avail. You become angry and indignant with a similar unsatisfying outcome. This exhausts your usual repertoire of options when you are faced with situations such as this. You shrug in defeat and begin to walk away.

Something in you breaks loose. Maybe it is because you are tired after your long journey, or that you are feeling especially desperate, or that you don't see other choices, but something, some inner strength, or perhaps insanity, pushes you over the edge. You turn back to the hotel clerk with a fierceness in your face that visibly shakes him. Before you open your mouth to speak, you can see he is terrified by what you are about to do—a course of action that even you are not yet sure about. When you finally let loose, it is with a steely calmness that is even more unsettling than the scream the clerk was expecting. You explain that you wish to see the manager, that you have no intention of sleeping anywhere else except in this very facility. If they can't find a room for you, then you'll simply have to sleep in the lobby. As you utter this last declaration, your eyes fall on a large, overstuffed couch. "There!" you announce, pointing at your bed for the evening. "I shall sleep right here."

Before you can begin to unpack your bags, all before an increasingly large and amused audience, an assistant manager presses a key into your hand. "Please," he says pleadingly, "let me show you to your room."

The significant aspect of this little scenario is not the way an assertive outburst got you what you wanted but the valuable lesson you learned, which you can apply to many other aspects of your life. From childhood, we are taught not to make scenes, to be good little girls and boys and then proper young ladies and gracious gentlemen. Here, however, you found that you did have the capacity to demand satisfaction—and that this new sense of power was very enjoyable indeed.

Could you have learned this lesson in a context other than traveling? Naturally. But it is under circumstances in which you are without usual cues and support, in strange surroundings, vulnerable and raw, that you are often willing to resort to more creative solutions to the problems that confront you.

Becoming Adaptable

In describing the way in which change, once begun, carries forth a momentum that begets further change, Charles Dickens was amazed how quickly "what was rock before, becomes but sand and dust." It is the departure from familiarity, Dickens noted, that promotes confusion and disorientation, the conditions that make us most adaptable.

Human learning in general, and truly significant learning in particular, take place when you become adaptable. It is comical sometimes the extent to which we are willing to adapt to circumstances we find unusual.

One woman describes this story as an example of ways she changed after a journey to Southeast Asia. The trip became meaningful for her because she was forced to do things she had never imagined were possible.

Just before I went to Thailand this guy told me about this cobra that raised itself at him when he entered the toilet. That image stuck so fast that I had this little ritual when having to use the toilet in one of those out-of-the-way places. My ritual consisted of slapping my heel on the path and shouting, "Here I come, look out!" as I made my way, in the dark, to the toilet. Throwing open the door, I would then yell some more, hoping for the best. Sometimes the light was so dim it was impossible to know whether I was sharing my ablutions with a snake or a party of ten. However, anyone around must have thought I was one weird tourist.

Even as she laughed aloud while she was reminiscing about this experience, the woman nodded to herself as a reminder of the extent to which she could adapt to difficult situations. Ever since then, there have been times she has sat in meetings that have been downright vicious. Just when she feels herself withdrawing, or even thinking about bolting from the room, she remembers that this situation is nothing compared to that long, dark walk to the toilet.

Facing Fears

In almost any context, fear inhibits growth. While a certain degree of apprehension, even moderate anxiety, can motivate action, fear is a paralyzing emotion that leads to avoidance, inaction, or escape.

Fear is an integral part of transformative change, a companion as it were, especially if you are experimenting with new behaviors, facing novel challenges, putting yourself in difficult predicaments. Yet unless your specific fears are recognized, acknowledged, and worked through, very little in the way of growth is likely to take place.

Fear is not a single reaction but rather encompasses a variety of sensations, each alike in their suffocating nature that prevents constructive growth:

- *Fear of the unknown,* which makes you unwilling to place yourself in new situations, taste new foods, experiment with new ways of acting.

- *Fear of being alone,* which stops you from venturing forth on your own and visiting places that are of interest to you.

- *Fear of differences,* which leads you to feel threatened by people or customs that are dissimilar from what you are used to.

- *Fear of not being understood,* which can keep you from making an effort to communicate, especially when language barriers prevent you from expressing yourself as clearly as you would like.

- *Fear of failure,* which prevents you from trying new things, or even trying to speak local languages, because you are afraid you won't appear perfectly competent.

In each of these cases, but especially in the fear of failure, we confuse a single act with a label we bestow upon ourselves: Because I have failed in this one attempt, therefore, I am a failure. Deep down inside, most of us feel like impostors, if not frauds. However much we pretend to be confident, self-assured, capable, and secure, much of the time we are faking it. We don't know nearly as much as we pretend to others. Doubt is a constant condition of being alive.

Our fears and doubts must be brought under control, if not defeated, or we will never learn from our struggles, except to avoid risks in the future. When Helen Thayer attempted to become the first woman to walk to the magnetic North Pole alone, it was fear, not Arctic conditions, that she was conquering. Her journey was about surviving on her own, about dealing with physical challenges and discomforts, about finding her way in a stark place with few landmarks, about facing hungry polar bears.

"My first job," Thayer wrote in her journal after the first day, "was to conquer my fear and replace it with aggression so that I could stay under control, do whatever I had to do when confronted with danger."

A few days later, she had given the matter some more thought and decided that what makes a trip of this sort life-altering is the opportunities it provides to face that which is most difficult. "I wonder if the real definition of courage," Thayer wrote to herself, "is the ability to deal successfully with one's fears. At the end of this expedition I hope to be not only alive, but also able to say that I have courage."

This courage is a very individual sort of thing. For one traveler, going one on one with the Arctic is what it takes to provide a suitable test. For another, it is more than enough to leave a tour group for an afternoon, spending the time in solo exploration of a city. Each of us, however, must face our own polar bears, whether on the ice, in a back alley, or in a shopping mall.

Reflective Contemplation

Unless you spend time making sense of what happened to you, what you learned, and how you intend to capitalize on these lessons, any effects are likely to wane. While trying to sustain momentum, therapists often ask people to analyze what happened, why it happened in that particular way, how they are feeling and reacting to the situation, how they would prefer to respond differently, and finally, what they intend to do in the future. Such reflective time is equally important during powerful travel experiences.

Outward Bound, for example, designs its programs so that participants face graduated risks that are just beyond present skills. Participants also complete therapeutic tasks that produce emotional arousal and altered states of consciousness. Finally, leaders build into the experience opportunities for contemplative solitude so that there is time to create some meaning out of the experience.

One participant describes how this works:

We all skied along in single file, completely silent. Our guides warned us that we weren't allowed to speak at all, that they would signal when it was time for each of us to go off on our own. I was dropped off in my own valley in this wilderness area and promised that they would pick me up the next day.

After I set up camp, I had a number of writing assignments to complete, the most interesting of which was to write a letter to myself that the guides would keep and then mail to me six months later. In this letter, I wrote to myself about what I wanted to do differently in my life. I talked about changes that I decided to get going when I returned. I was very specific about all the goals that I wanted to reach and all the things I intended to do when I get back.

Then, I forgot all about the letter.

Sure enough, six months later, I went to pick up the mail and I saw that envelope written in my own handwriting. My heart started pounding as I remembered all the things I had declared I wanted to do with my life that day in my snowy, isolated valley. I ripped open the letter and saw, to my surprise, that I had completed almost every one of the goals I had wanted to reach. I also noticed that many of the conclusions I had reached on that day no longer seemed to fit my circumstances. I was relieved to see that I had indeed changed a lot since I had written that letter.

It should be noted with caution that whereas the exercise of trying to make sense of what happened is desirable, it's often difficult to come up with satisfying answers. In studies undertaken to assess the impact of Outward Bound travels, participants can quite easily describe *what* changes they experienced but not *why* they occurred.

One director of an Outward Bound program in Australia reported in a book by Renate Wilson that he is not the least surprised by the difficulty explaining the changes that take place: "People who have experienced Outward Bound exude a confidence bordering on faith. Since it is difficult to analyze faith, it is also difficult to analyze for whom and exactly why Outward Bound works."

Although the result of such contemplative activity may not result in definitive answers, the effort expended in trying to create meaning from experience seems to be crucial. Just as the participant who described his letter testified, the most memorable part of most adventure-based programs like Outward Bound is often the solo in which participants are dropped off in an isolated valley, mountaintop, meadow, or island, to fend for themselves for a few days while programmed to think about their lives and what they intend to do differently when they rejoin civilization.

Putting It All Together

Most of the elements just reviewed play a role in travel experiences that are transformative, just as they operate at powerful levels in any learning encounter. Imagine, for example, that you are walking around a strange city, diligently following your map to the local museum for your "canned culture." Unexpectedly, you find yourself lost. You feel confused, frustrated, scared, and a little excited by this unintended challenge *(emotional arousal)*. You now realize that the day is not going to follow your agenda, but rather than feeling disappointed, you revel in the freedom to do something out of character—to wander around a bit and see what happens *(perception of freedom)*. This is new territory for you, not usually part of the ways you operate. There is a perception of danger and adventure, although you recognize you are probably overreacting a bit *(facing fears)*. Nevertheless, you feel open to whatever might come your way.

Sure enough, in no time you find yourself talking to a variety of different people trying to find out where you are, and where you might go next. You are surprised by how open people are to you, how friendly and helpful they are. Then you wonder if they might just be responding so well to you because *you* feel so friendly and open. After all, experiences like this don't ever seem to happen when you are home *(situational change)*.

The day goes by all too quickly. You have seen nothing of the museums and the tourist spots but you have met a dozen new people. You have learned something of their customs, just as you have revealed yourself to them. The smells and tastes and images of the day linger soothingly at the edge of your mind *(altered state of consciousness)*. This was not just an ordinary day in your life. You attach great meaning to what transpired. You are proud of the ways you adapted to the changing circumstances. You did not pout or complain or berate yourself. You just went with the flow. You muse about ways you might operate this way more often when you get home *(reflective contemplation)*.

—⁓—

This is just one day in a person's life, yet a good example of how travel can be so stimulating when you make an effort to push yourself beyond usual patterns. All these ingredients come together in a systematic process that forms the backbone of lasting change.

6

Refashioning Yourself

*Y*ou have planned a trip that has the potential to change some aspect of your existence. This could involve altering your appearance, your relationships, your values and attitudes, your habits and behavior, or perhaps your plans for the future. Depending on the particular goals you have in mind, you are now ready to focus your attention on specific facets of your travel experience.

One of the things traveling does is take you away from your normal environment and from the continuous expectations that others have for you. It is under such circumstances that it's possible to refashion yourself into another person. When you're traveling nobody really knows the way you are supposed to be. You can experiment with new roles and alternative personas. You can quite literally become a different person from the one who left home.

To promote such dramatic changes, you need to know what options are available. You may readily agree that people are different when they're on vacation but exactly *how* are they different? What is it about your state of consciousness, your very state of being, that makes you so much more susceptible to being influenced by the people, places, and events swirling around you when you are traveling?

HEIGHTENED SENSES DURING TRAVEL

It is possible to refashion yourself on a trip in ways that would be far more difficult at home because of the different filters you employ to perceive the world and how you are interacting with it. For example, you are far more flexible and suggestible when traveling. Your senses are altered as well—not just your faculties of sight, smell, hearing, and touch, but also your sense of time, space, history, play, connectedness to others, even your sense of self.

Talk to someone after he returns from an especially powerful journey and you will be bombarded by vivid descriptions of each of these sense-based experiences. It becomes altogether clear that one reason why the trip was so transformative was because the traveler attended to things that ordinarily escape awareness.

I spoke with a teacher who had just returned from a memorable sojourn abroad. When I asked her what it was about the trip that felt so important to her, she hesitated for only a moment before she started talking. Once she began, it was like a whole barrage of images tumbled forth at amazing speed:

> There's all that excitement and anticipation and nervousness at the outset. There's all the challenge of a new culture, language, morals, transport, ways of being understood and getting what you need. There's all the powerful learning about yourself, what you exist on, what you put up with, how incredibly giving human beings can be, how conniving others can be. There is the delight in difference and contrast—unusual flora, customs, fabrics, tastes. You take less for granted. You realize heaps about your own culture and how bizarre some of your own habits are. You are forced out of yourself to consider assumptions you take for granted. You are also able to make those links with new experiences that make sense of the past in new ways, unexpected ways. Time gets looped. Themes emerge. Sights become sharp and surreal. Ahhhhhhhhhh. I wish I was off again now somewhere new—

It was at this point that I had to intervene. She was off and running at such blazing speed that I couldn't keep up with her. There were just so many ways her senses had been stimulated in so many different dimensions. Next time you take a trip, you'd be well advised to examine more closely how your senses are affected at each of these levels.

Sense of Time

When you are in the midst of a journey, time becomes slower, or faster, but rarely progresses at a pace that seems familiar. Wherever you go, the perception of time changes drastically according to whom you are with, what you are doing, and what is customary for that locale. Time slows down and speeds up in ways that are jarring. A journey on a crowded, bumpy plane or a rocking ship can seem interminable. An hour can last a day, a day a whole week. Other times, when you are completely engaged in an activity, time rockets along at a pace that hardly seems fair. Once you finally get into the swing of things, the ride seems over all too quickly.

During the best of travel, time flows at a pace and rhythm all its own. When you are riveted by a sunset, the cadence of waves crashing onto the beach, the chaotic melody of a street market, or a fascinating conversation, time seems to stop altogether.

Even boredom during travel has its uses. What distinguishes the true traveler, according to Aldous Huxley, is the appreciation of boredom "not merely philosophically, but almost with pleasure." It is part of the whole experience, the counterpoint to bursts of excitement, the parentheses that hold within them the one nugget of exaltation that defines the whole trip.

Another lesson you learn during a trip is how you can recalibrate your sense of time depending on what is customary for that area. To a Swiss German, time is measured precisely, obeyed without question. To a Peruvian, time is but an elastic boundary, stretched to fit the activity of the moment. Even within North America, the differences in time perception are striking. In Savannah or Charleston or Charlottesville, the past is all important; in parts of the Paiute reservation, the inner city of Detroit, or the Los Angeles barrio, there is only the present, and a bleak one at that; in Westchester, Orange, or Fairfax counties, parents look primarily to the future for their children. In Las Vegas or Atlantic City casinos, time has a different meaning altogether, one without clocks or windows to signal when it is time to eat or sleep.

Notice the differences in the ways you relate to time when you are on a trip. Pay attention, in particular, to how you would like to change the patterns and structure of your sense of time. During your trip, for example, you experience such rapture as a result of slowing time down to appreciate how wonderful it feels to stay focused on what's happening in any moment.

Back home, a week later, you are hurrying from your car to some scheduled event, walking briskly, filled with nervous energy, repeatedly checking your watch, thinking about a hundred different things except what you are doing in that moment. You stop and smile to yourself, remembering how different time felt walking on the beach a week ago. You take a deep breath and deliberately slow down. You make a point to notice where you are and what's going on around you.

You arrive at your appointment an extra minute late, but with a newfound sense of serenity. All this is possible because of how you refashioned your sense of time.

Sense of History

People in various parts of the world relate not only to present time in various ways but also to connections to their past. There is a pervasive feeling of history associated with walking around Athens, Rome, and Cairo that isn't there in Las Vegas, a place where age is measured in decades rather than centuries. Similarly, geological time shapes your whole attitude, mood, and perception of your surroundings. Relatively young places like New Zealand or the Big Island of Hawaii feel distinctly different from more geologically settled continents like Australia or the eastern coast of North America.

People, as well, have a different consciousness about history. If in Rome, you do as the Romans do, then the same thing is true in Bali, Nairobi, or Miami. Your perceptions of time and appreciation of history are altered every place you go, making you more or less aware of your place in the world as compared to others who lived before you.

A Canadian woman told me of a visit to her ancestral home of Scotland, still absolutely chilled by the feeling of history she encountered in each spot her family might have once frequented: "I dropped into Scotland like a nut onto a bolt. My circuits were charged in Glasgow, overloaded by Edinburgh, and short-circuited in St. Andrews. I was sitting on the balcony of a house overlooking the seventeenth tee when quite suddenly I felt as though someone had thrown a mantle over me. I could feel it settling over me quite physically, and found myself saying to myself I don't have to leave this place. I don't ever have to leave."

Many people travel to find their family or cultural roots, or to reconnect to a part of their past. Travel agents even specialize in organizing trips for African Americans to visit Ghana or war veterans to return to the sites of major battles. In these and many other sorts of travel, the ultimate outcome that results is an altered sense of history, not only about the world but about your own particular place in it.

Sense of Space

What a different feeling is elicited standing in the middle of the Gobi or Mohave deserts, as opposed to the rain forests of Malaysia or Brazil, or the low country of South Carolina versus the high sierra of Tahoe, or an island in remote Fiji instead of midtown Manhattan.

If geological time affects our perceptions of what is going on around us, so does geography. We thrive on this change of scenery. People find their moods changed drastically from the moment they arrive in a place. Languid, steamy, lush tropics. Brisk, clear, cold mountain air. Bristling energy radiating from a big city. The sense of space affects our priorities, our interests and needs, our very sense of self in relation to others.

For example, a city slicker who had never spent much time in wilderness areas decided to go on an organized backpacking trip in an isolated part of New Mexico. More than anything else, it was the total quiet of the mountains, the vast open spaces, that led him to think about how overscheduled and complex his life had become.

One morning I was hovered over my trench, doing my regular constitutional in the woods, when I had a flash as to what I was really doing there thirty miles from any other people besides my companions. All this discomfort and inconvenience of walking fifteen miles per day, carrying a load on my back like a mule, has been necessary for me to clear my head. I realized this as I was planning what I would do for the next two minutes, step by step. Unroll the toilet paper. Cover my tracks. And so on. I had no time to think about anything else. Every part of my existence was centered around dealing with the basics of staying alive—putting food into my body, drinking, peeing, purifying water, putting up the tent, drying my clothes, caring for my feet, carrying water, preparing meals, cleaning up, one thing after another. Everything else in my life, all my worries and ambitions, pale in comparison. They just don't matter here in this wild country.

Sense of Self

The self is a curious entity, at once an embodiment of all that is you and a construction of imagination that has no definable form. The self is your present sense of consciousness, an ever-changing form that is influenced continuously by everything around you.

As you travel from one place to another, your sense of self takes on various roles—intrepid explorer, dependent spouse, impatient child, judgmental American, guilty parent, naive tourist, cynical veteran, expert negotiator, helpless prisoner, tedious bore. None of these are really you, yet they are all different selves that make up part of the complete package.

The views you have of who you are, not to mention the perception of others, change constantly as you relocate yourself in space and time. In some places and situations, you see yourself as capable and adaptable; in others you feel quite incompetent. Imagine, for example, the different image you would portray to others, as well as the sense of self you would feel inside, as you:

- Hang on for dear life to a raft barreling down class IV rapids of the Salmon River.
- Make small talk at a formal dinner party in honor of a visiting dignitary.
- Walk through the streets of downtown Pittsburgh at night.
- Face the prospect of an eighteen-mile steep ascent to the top of an unstable volcano.
- Address an audience of six hundred people who are expecting to be entertained and informed.
- Intervene decisively to settle a dispute between people who are arguing.
- Check under the hood of your stalled vehicle to determine the cause of the malfunction that has stranded you on a deserted road.
- Convince an airline representative that you should be allowed to board an oversold flight.
- Calm down an overwrought child.

Each of these situations requires a different mindset and set of skills to deal effectively with it. In some of them you have little difficulty picturing yourself in a confident and competent role. Others make you shudder at even the prospect of facing such challenges.

What traveling teaches you is to expand your repertoire of selves. You learn to take on new roles, to try out alternative selves, thus gaining valuable experience. When you return, your sense of self is forever altered in light of what you lived through.

A woman in her fifties who had never been active athletically, decided to plan a trip to Rwanda to see the mountain gorillas that inhabit the region:

> I bought my first pair of hiking boots and broke them in as best I could walking around my neighborhood. The first day out in the bush was a breeze. We found a gorilla after a half hour, pleasant walk. I thought to myself this was really no big deal. I felt so confident and wondered what I had been so worried about.
>
> The second day we set off with our guides and porters. My porter had these red boots and they became my lifeline as we sloshed through mud and dense jungle. I didn't care about my husband or anyone else, just never letting those red boots out of my sight.
>
> We walked on and on all day, up mountains, through thickets and swamps. It was hot. It was exhausting. I couldn't believe I was doing this! I didn't stop. I didn't quit. I didn't get scared. I was so exhilarated that I was actually doing this!
>
> After about ten or twelve miles walking we finally saw the gorillas. And they were truly amazing to watch. So close too. As exciting as this was, that wasn't what was transformative for me. The big deal was that I was able to do this, to move through it, to challenge myself, to deal with the obstacles and discomfort. It was an unbelievable ordeal, one that I survived.

I asked her what was so meaningful about this experience. She knew immediately what was involved and that it had to do with changing the way she defined herself now as a rugged, intrepid explorer with a great capacity for physical discomfort. "I learned that it was possible for me to do so much more than I ever imagined, not just in trekking through jungles but in every other area of my life. Even today, eight years after this experience, I still feel changes rippling through me. I am now more physically active than ever before. Even approaching age sixty I no longer accept limitations that I have always lived with."

Sense of Connectedness

Some trips highlight how alone you feel in the world, whereas others infuse you with a spirit of connection to others. Although novelist Robertson Davies hates traveling, which he equates with being seasick or airsick, he does admit that a different sort of social rules apply to journeys, especially aboard ships. "Something about sea travel promotes intimacy," he observes, not at all sure he likes it. "People offer confidences, and are impudently intrusive, in a way that would never pass muster on land."

Why is it that people tell us things on airplanes, trains, and boats that they would never confide to their best friends back home? The answer, of course, is the perception that it is safe to do so. Seatmates have no past, nor probably any future.

One of the consequences of disengaging from your normal life is that you end up finding out who is most important to you. You become aware who you miss and who you don't. You learn about your own abilities to meet new people, as well as your tolerance for being in your own company.

Travel either brings you closer to others or moves you further apart. In most cases, you end up making new friends and building new contacts, as well as creating greater intimacy with those you are with. Ask a couple, *any* couple, when they have felt the closest to one another and often the time that comes to mind is one in which they faced obstacles together on the road, or even more likely, after recovering from such ordeals.

Legends are created from these trials under fire. That which does not destroy you makes you stronger. In other words, if frustration is kept under reasonable control, people frequently talk affectionately and wistfully about their difficult travels. They giggle as they tell stories of mishaps and misadventures. They grow closer as a result of their shared misery.

The classic example of this is understood in terms of what happens to soldiers in battle. Like the critical travel ordeal, one would never choose to be placed in dangerous or trying predicaments; yet foxholes make fast friends.

I recall the disastrous day my wife and I lived through on our twentieth anniversary. Yet I tell this story with a smile, grateful for what the experience offered us. We were in the Philippines, mainly as tourists but also available to consult with local universities. In exchange for our services, one college offered to take us to the beach for the day. My wife and I were delighted, not just to see some of the countryside, but to be in the company of local people who would be our guides.

When they showed up in a jeepney, a kind of souped-up truck they use for public transport, we were a little leery but climbed aboard. We were told the ride would take about two hours so we gritted our teeth, held on for our lives, and bounced around on back roads that made us feel like we were inside a blender. The driver got lost and it took us seven excruciating hours to reach our destination, sick, hot, hungry, aching, and miserable. Then it started to rain.

Throughout the ordeal we took turns boosting one another's spirits. There was no sense complaining or whining—we had no choice but to hang on and go wherever they took us. In some sense, the whole thing was comical. We each reminded one another what a great story it would make, an anniversary we would never forget.

The driver promised us he would take a short cut home. Another seven hours later, this time in stop-and-go Manila traffic, clogged with exhaust fumes so thick you could almost grab particles out of the air, we finally arrived back at our hotel, exhausted and wasted. We thanked our hosts for their hospitality, unwilling to offend them or appear ungracious. After they drove off, we began giggling hysterically. This had been one of the most miserable days of our lives, yet it was utterly unforgettable. We had survived. Furthermore, we felt much closer to one another, an intimacy that only strengthened our relationship. If we could get through this together, we could meet most any future challenge in a similar spirit of good cheer. In fact, the next day we flew on to Hong Kong, crossing the international date line and thereby allowing us to celebrate our anniversary again under more comfortable circumstances.

Not only can travel bond partners closer together, it can also make us feel a closer connection to the people of a particular locale, to feel that we belong among them as a citizen of the world. Whether you are hanging out in a Dublin pub, a playground in Kansas City, a train station in Turkey, a beach in Cancun, or a racetrack in Melbourne, there are times when you feel like you are so much a part of the scene, so accepted and enamored by the locals, that you feel a greater sense of connection to the world and all its inhabitants.

Sense of Play

This transformative business seems like it is all work. It's about doing things you don't really want to do. It's about thinking hard about stuff you would rather leave alone. It's about making mountains out of molehills, and molehills out of mountains.

Yet travel is primarily about play. It means letting go of work, at least as we usually think about it. Screenwriter David Mamet tells of being on vacation with his family in the Caribbean. He was sitting on the beach, which reminded him of Joseph Conrad and Somerset Maugham, and thinking profound thoughts, finding metaphors and similes in everything. Always the writer, searching for dialogue that might end up in his next *Glengary Glen Ross,* he lay on the beach and *pretended* to relax. Really, though, he was always working, thinking, transforming—that is, until his daughter called out to him: "My daughter asked me to come out and make 'flour,' and rather than responding 'Just a minute' I went out and made flour. Making flour consisted of pouring sand onto a palm leaf, and I was surprised to find it quite as enjoyable as (and certainly more productive than) a business lunch at the Russian Tea Room."

There is indeed a time for play, for not thinking. Increased freedom and flexibility result mainly from giving up the work structures that usually rule your life. One purpose of vacations is to remind you how much fun it is to let yourself go. This experience is even more useful when you can refashion your sense of play after you return to the world of work.

Sense of Cause-Effect

Last, but hardly least important, are changes that take place as a result of learning that things are not always as they seem. When traveling, you are often able to refashion your perceptions of what causes certain things to happen, a shift that may produce some dramatic changes in other areas of your life.

Each of us has some fairly distinct assumptions about what causes things to happen. Snow showers are caused by weather fronts moving in from the west. Riots are caused by civil unrest. Stomachaches result from drinking unpurified water. Delayed flights are caused by the aforementioned snow showers.

We embrace these beliefs so readily, and have them confirmed so frequently by others of our kind, that we rarely consider how tenuous our hold is on perceptions of reality. For example, one traveler returned from a serious mission to Guatemala to learn all she could about textile weaving. She spent weeks learning all she could from local artisans, eventually joining them in the creation of her own products. She had been making steady progress in her craft until one dye lot of wool became completely spoiled. The woman wondered what exactly had caused the problem. Perhaps it was some impurity in the material, or too much of a specific ingredient. Maybe, she mused further, she had stirred the dye too vigorously or too timidly. She even considered the increased humidity as a possible culprit.

When she brought her ruined garment to one of the older, experienced members of the guild, the Guatemalan woman nodded immediately. "It's the full moon," she explained. "You must wait a few days before you begin another batch of dye."

The traveler walked away, more than a little puzzled by this explanation, so she decided to seek a second opinion from another local whose work she admired. When her consultant began laughing uproariously, giggling completely out of control, the woman felt an immediate sense of relief, at least until she heard the alternative explanation: "That's utterly ridiculous. Of course the full moon has nothing to do with ruining your dye. It must be a pregnant woman nearby."

When the woman returned home from Guatemala, she had learned a lot about weaving, but not nearly as much as she learned about perceptions of reality. Ever since that encounter she was forever shifting her perceptions to consider alternative ways of viewing any situation. More than anything she had ever read, studied, or done before, she found that being able to look at the same problem from different angles allowed her to increase her creativity tenfold. While she didn't believe that her dye had actually been spoiled by a full moon or passing pregnant woman, she did realize at that moment that an infinite number of explanations could be equally valid. She felt the platform of her thinking collapse just then, a foundation she determined never to construct so rigidly again.

This woman's lesson confirms a principle that British author G. K. Chesterton discovered at the turn of the century: the object of travel is not to see foreign lands but to see your own country as a foreign land. An Italian American woman, for example, had long viewed her native Italy as an exotic and intriguing place, that is, until she finally returned from America for a visit:

> I enjoyed my vacation and the chance I had to meet many relatives I didn't even know I had. Overall, though, I was disappointed. Italy did not live up to what I had expected. I felt uncomfortable much of the

time. Everything was foreign to me. Italian families function so differently. I was shocked by the sexism. As a woman, I felt truly oppressed.

This trip was an eye-opening experience for me. I kept missing the conveniences back home, the music, and even the food. Upon returning home, I felt instantly patriotic in ways I never could have imagined. It felt so great to be back home! Years later, I still feel grateful for what I learned during that journey—to appreciate more what I have and where I live.

—⁓—

There is often a shift in perception that takes place when you spend time in a strange culture. It is in the act of noting differences regarding the ways people think and express themselves, attribute causes to phenomena, and carry out their lives that you are able to view your own life from a new perspective.

7

Focusing on People

There is much to be said about the value of a special environment away from home to help you gain some perspective on your life. Indeed, some of the most magical moments you can ever recall may have been spent sitting on a pristine beach, walking through the streets of a vibrant city, or viewing the countryside from a mountain perch.

Even the names of certain spots on Earth—Tahiti, Surfers Paradise, Disneyland, Serengeti, Corfu, Zion, London—bring to mind the prospect of a perfect vacation. Upon returning from a trip to such popular tourist spots it is common for people to remark about what a great place it was and what a delightful time they had. "You should go there," they will plead, "it's wonderful!"

Transformative travel results as much from your interactions with people as it does from your response to the physical setting. Whether you go to Bangladesh or Cleveland, the Black Forest or Central Park, the Caspian Sea or the Great Salt Lake, there is equal potential for your experience to be memorable, depending on the people you are with along the way.

PERSONAL CONNECTIONS

Experienced travelers have discovered that what makes a trip most memorable is not the places you visit but the people with whom you come into close contact. One woman who has been around the world and back several times remarks about the strategy she has developed:

> When I travel, I always learn something about the country or place that I'm visiting. It's educational learning about the geography, the resources, the art, the history, the rituals, the culture. Then there's also the process, the connections, the interactions that happen between me and others. It's this second part that I consider to be far more meaningful and memorable.
>
> My husband and I work hard to seek out people when we travel, to learn about their daily life. We make a human connection with a place. That connection between people of different cultures and experiences is the most enriching part of travel for us.
>
> I could go to the most exquisite, magical place in the world, or visit seven museums and eleven churches, but it wouldn't be nearly as interesting to me if I didn't make friends with someone who could act as a guide to her world.
>
> That's why I love going to marketplaces because that's a place where it is so easy to make connections. Whether I speak the language or not, it doesn't matter because we can communicate with gestures or our eyes and smiles. There are just so many faces that come to mind right now—in Burma, in South Africa, in Thailand, in New Guinea, in Kashmir, of these interactions I've had with people—with adults but especially with children. For that reason I bring candy and a Polaroid camera with me so I can give gifts to children of their own pictures.
>
> I can't even pick a peak experience because there are so many. What they all have in common is that we meet people. We are invited into their homes. We meet their families. We exchange gifts. There is a bond that develops and is felt by all of us. I come away enriched and touched and moved for having known these people.
>
> Once I have seen how another culture lives, I take some of that and incorporate it into my life. Rituals are so important for every phase of life's events. I have borrowed some of these practices and integrated

them into my family or my work. For example, we use a kind of candle-lighting ceremony at our dinner table on special occasions that we had seen practiced in another part of the world.

I feel so filled with experiences. There are just so many people I've met along the way. I am grateful for each one of them. I feel touched.

What this woman is describing is a kind of travel that is anchored not by where she is but by whom she is with. She's describing a kind of travel that is marked by connections to people rather than to places. Places do make some difference, but they are far less important than most people think if the intent is to promote personal change.

Who, Not Where

It does not matter where you go but rather how and with whom you go. "One's destination is never a place," writes Henry Miller, "but rather a new way of looking at things."

It is absurd when people say that Chicago is lovely but Detroit is not, or that you must see Thailand but not Bali, or that Australia is much friendlier than New Zealand. A destination is simply a stopping place to immerse yourself in the experimental process of questioning yourself. This often happens as a direct result of your interactions with others you meet.

Travel to new places, or even working in strange cultures, forces us to develop greater flexibility as we challenge our most cherished beliefs about the way things should be. When I teach, for example, I have always been fond of a fairly organized classroom. I believe learning takes place best when I can control the environment for my students, sequence progressive activities, and create an atmosphere that is exciting but also safe.

Once, however, I was invited to Hawaii to work with several groups of teachers. My job was to offer a course on counseling skills that I have taught previously a hundred different times. I have each segment meticulously planned and can anticipate most everything that might occur.

Nothing, however, prepared me for my delightful yet chaotic group in Maui. Picture this: about twenty-five experienced teachers, representing a number of cultures—Filipino, Japanese, Malay, Native Hawaiian, and even a few mainlanders—are sitting in the room listening to me talk about some innovative discipline strategy. Mostly listening, anyway. For if you were to peek into the room you would see me pacing around as I speak, holding in my arms a three-month-old baby, the child of one of the students. His crib is located in the back of the room where he stays during class most of the time, except when he's crying. Now it's my turn to entertain him, a task I am greatly enjoying even if his babbling is distracting my train of thought. Not nearly as much, though, as the staccato bursts from the police radio calling out reports from the squad car parked near the door. You see, the Maui police officer attending the class may have to rush out at a moment's notice to stop some crime in progress.

I can tune out the radio at times, the baby's squalling at other times, but there are two other children in attendance, ages five and eight, who are cramping my style because now I have to watch my language. In fact, at various times there is a perpetual army of kids and family members coming in and out, delivering food, messages, or just plain curious about what we are up to.

If the auditory distractions are challenging, then certain visual images are just as arresting. Just in front of me a shop teacher is disassembling the light housing from his Harley motorcycle, trying to get it to work before he drives home. *Everyone* is in the process of eating something; fingers, forks, chopsticks are blazing. All the while I'm talking, I'm scoping out what looks good. I reach out and pop a sushi into my mouth while I'm waiting for someone to answer a question.

This is my classroom in Maui, a wonderful scene, beyond anything I could ever have imagined. My colleagues back home would be appalled at the chaos, disgusted by the lack of discipline and order, bemused by what would be labeled as low academic standards. But wow! This is a fun way to teach and learn! The support and caring in the room is incredible.

When class ends, the students feel so grateful for my efforts. I'm certain, though, that I learned far more than they did. I never realized I could be so adaptive, and that by letting go of my preconceptions, such amazing things could happen. It feels like many things I thought were important about teaching really don't matter. There is an essence to the process that transcends crying babies, police radios, clinking motorcycle parts, and Captain Crunch cereal.

If I am different as a result of my trip, it wasn't because of the long runs along the beach, the hikes in the volcanic crater, the snorkeling and scuba diving, the shopping and sightseeing. All of those activities were wonderful and entertaining and relaxing—but they didn't transform me in any enduring way. What made the greatest difference were the conversations with people I met. I learned about lifestyles radically different from my own. I saw my own world through other eyes. I tested cherished beliefs in a context that made them obsolete. I felt a closeness to other people. These were the things that changed me.

Cultural Challenges

Every culture presents us with new challenges to figure out how to communicate properly and how to get our needs met without being offensive. This is exactly the value of cross-cultural friendships. Whether a marriage between a Catholic and a Jew, a friendship between an Italian American and a Mexican American, or a working relationship among people of varied ethnic, religious, and cultural groups, such interactions teach us about other ways of making sense of the world.

Sometimes we are reluctant students, initially uninterested in the characters around us. We are deluded into thinking that the real action is in the gorgeous scenery outside the window instead of the people sitting right next to us. One traveler describes the moment he discovered that the people were far more transformative than the place:

> I was sitting on a bus, nervously trying to calculate at which stop I should get off to see the park that was supposed to be so beautiful. I was feeling proud of my decision to take public transport in a strange city when I could have easily taken a taxi, or gotten someone to drive me. I was also feeling annoyed by the old man sitting next to me who insisted on talking when I much preferred to be left alone.
>
> In spite of my best efforts to discourage him, the man kept a running commentary about something or other. I was hardly listening. At one point, he stopped talking and looked at me. He had apparently asked me a question and was waiting patiently for an answer. With a sigh, I gave up my views of the city flowing by and joined him in some sort of discussion.
>
> What a kick this old guy was! He entertained me with stories of his days in the army. He talked about the history of his city. He captivated me with his warmth and charm. I found it ironic that of everything I did and saw during my visit, the most memorable thing of all was sitting on the bus talking to this old man.

We can learn so much from the people around us when we are traveling. It is their views, opinions, and perspectives that teach us the most about alternative ways to look at things, often those we had not considered before. Why does this not happen more when we are home? Why don't we have as many positive, intriguing conversations during our normal lives?

For one thing, we are more open to others when on vacation. For another, we are more relaxed. And just as we are intrigued by differences in people and customs, finding them exotic and cute, so too do others find our accent and manner engaging. Although we may think of our fellow citizens as rude and insensitive and our community as a fairly inhospitable place, visitors may get quite a different impression, just as you might in their town.

An Australian is astounded by the politeness he sees whenever he visits North America. "Wait a minute," I say. "You're kidding?"

"No, no," he insists passionately. "Everyone says 'you're welcome' and 'Have a nice day'—often as if they really mean it. In my country they'd just sneer or maybe say 'Fuck off' under their breath."

Of course it is precisely because he is a stranger, with an exotic accent, that he is treated so graciously. This would be the case, as well, if you or I were a guest in his country. Basically, people like to talk to foreign visitors. They want to show off their community. Most of all, though, they want to learn about life elsewhere. It is just so stimulating to talk to people around the world who think in different ways.

TRAVELING LIKE AN ANTHROPOLOGIST

If the tourist touches only the most superficial aspects of a culture, and the traveler digs much deeper to really experience aspects of the new place at first hand, then the anthropologist delves deeper still into what a culture and its people are all about. Ethnographic methods have been developed in which a visitor enters a culture as a *participant-observer*. This means that you join the host culture, become part of daily rituals and activities as a native; at the same time, you watch carefully what is going on around you. You are an insider in manner and dress, yet remain an outsider in your reflections about what you observe and experience.

To join a culture and see it from the inside, you must first be accepted by its people. Anthropologist Clifford Geertz tells the story of how he was able to gain entrance into the normally elusive Balinese society, a world closed off to most outsiders. He had been watching a cockfight that was raided by police. Rather than identifying himself to authorities as a tourist and receiving special treatment, he chose to flee and hide with the Balinese. After that reckless choice, he was accepted by them as an equal.

As a participant-observer in a culture, you are constantly making inferences about the place you are visiting. You increase your awareness of the behavior around you, as well as the tacit cultural rules, by using what anthropologist James Spradley called a "wide angle lens." You are looking at the big picture to find the meaning that a particular activity has for local people. You study some of the cultural contradictions of the place—why, for example, in our own country people say things like "Glad to meet you!" when they really aren't.

Like an anthropologist, you can look at the way conflict is managed, the way status is acquired and maintained, or the way problems are solved. You can examine several dimensions of space (How do people use their land and dwellings?), objects (What things do people value most?), activities (What do people do at various times?), goals (What is most important for people to achieve and how do they do that?), and feelings (How do people describe and express their emotions?).

As an anthropologist, you have two paradoxical goals, each of which makes the other more difficult. On one side, you attempt full and complete engagement with all people and opportunities that come your way. You "go native"—eat the foods, speak the language, practice the customs, even try to think as your new friends and neighbors do. Yet pulling at you from the other side is the goal to be an objective, analytic observer of events. Your job is to see as clearly as you can exactly what is happening. Then the hard part: to figure out the underlying meaning of the events you witnessed. You are thus being subjective and objective at the same time, a predicament that can give anyone a headache.

One time, I was sitting in a small café located on the grounds of an Aboriginal reservation in Northern Australia. The restaurant was just outside the local high school and catered to the few children and many teachers who could afford lunch. While chomping away on a sandwich filled with some unidentified substance (I was recalling the greatest delicacy among traditional people in the bush is the grub worm), I witnessed an interaction that seemed, at first, quite inconsequential.

The white manager had his back to us, frying heaps of onions. The cashier, an Aboriginal girl, was chatting with an older man who was huddled with her to the side. While they were thus engaged, a line of customers began to form, patiently waiting to be served. The girl continued her conversation oblivious to the line of people that was growing longer by the minute.

The manager then turned to her and curtly asked her to finish the conversation another time. Seemed reasonable to me, I thought. But the old man, who turned out to be her father, was greatly offended by this interruption: "How dare you talk to her like that!"

To my surprise, the manager quickly backed down, apologizing with the lame excuse he was only doing his job. The father was not to be pacified. He abruptly turned and walked out of the store. The girl then began serving the waiting customers.

What was *that* all about, I wondered? Obviously, some sort of cultural misunderstanding. What else could the poor guy have done, I asked myself? Was he supposed to let the restaurant fill up with impatient customers while the cashier chatted with her father? Through my eyes as a cultural observer, I could have seen no other alternative. It seemed to me that the daughter was irresponsible and that the father overreacted.

I decided to check things out with Aboriginal teachers I had been sitting with. They, after all, witnessed the same interaction and noticed my curiosity about the scene.

Their impression turned out to be quite different from mine. They figured the manager should have kept frying his onions and left the girl alone.

"But what about all the impatient people waiting in line?" I pointed out incredulously.

"Were they really impatient?" they asked me in return. "To us, they looked quite content to wait as long as it took for the girl to finish her conversation. That man showed disrespect to the father, who was right to be angry about it."

Again I queried: "But what about the customers?"

"Look," they explained carefully. "If it bothered them very much then *they* might have asked the father's permission to have the daughter's attention. For the white man to interrupt was wrong. If it bothered him so much that customers were waiting then *he* should have helped them. After all, he was only frying onions whereas she was talking to her father."

It is a magical experience to consider alternative ways of viewing a single incident. When you seek to understand how local people see the same events in ways that are radically different, it forces you to consider other options that are possible, not just with that one situation but with anything else in the future. Once you get outside of your own parochial, self-centered attitudes, other possibilities emerge.

What is the value of such perceptual shifts? They're like stretching exercises for the mind. In other situations when you find yourself stuck, you can make similar changes in the way you view your predicament, alterations that can provide options that you might never otherwise consider.

Being a Snoop

Whether you think like an anthropologist or not, it does help to be nosy. A crucial part of intrepid travel is being a curious investigator, asking lots of questions to discover what lies beneath the surface. Relentless in your search, you are trying to find out why things are the way they are.

Traveler Jonathan Raban is addicted to the call of a good adventure, finding that being a snoop is the best part of his role. Although back home he is a shy recluse, a grump by his own admission, when on the road he can't help asking impertinent questions: "How long does it take to learn to play the nose-flute?" or "So how did you come to lose your other leg?"

A word of caution is in order, however. Raban finds that when you ask such questions you have to be prepared for the consequences: "The world is littered with travelers who asked one question too many, got a satisfactory answer and never went home again."

Hearing Stories

We are changed not only by the experiences we live but also by the stories we hear from others. That is the attraction, after all, of the movies and books we devour—the opportunity to live other lives vicariously, as well as to be touched deeply by such secondary excursions.

It is one thing to hear a sanitized, polished story, as orchestrated by the author or director. It is an altogether more powerful jolt to hear the real thing in the protagonist's own voice.

When traveling, you hear lots of these moving stories that expand your world—from companions who reveal new parts of themselves, from fellow travelers you meet along the road who haunt you with their tales of woe or romance, from the local people you meet along the way. This is even the case with tour guides who are deputized by their communities to entertain visitors.

Jimmy is one such guide who has been leading trips through his native Kalaupapa, the infamous leper colony on the island of Molokai. One of the last remaining residents of the colony established by a Hawaiian king in the beginning of the eighteenth century, he was sent there to die as a young boy. While he dutifully takes guests on a tour of this isolated peninsula, walled in by the highest sea cliffs in the world, you are captivated not so much by the historical sites and picturesque churches, or even by one of the most remote and beautiful spots anywhere, as by Jimmy's own life story.

As he talks about being taken from his family at age thirteen to be exiled with people who were crippled and disfigured, or being unable to hold or touch his own children for fear of giving them his disease, you are aware of your own heart pounding in sympathy. Memories of the perfect beach and turquoise water may fade. Souvenir T-shirts will wear out. But you will never forget the stories you have heard from people who have had such different lives from your own.

Keeping an Open Mind

The change process being described, through its various phases, reflects the cultural filters from which you examine your own actions, as well as those of other people with whom you come into contact. Kevin, an architect who travels widely throughout Asia supervising the construction of hotels and office complexes, typifies the attitude that many Westerners feel as they look at other cultures through ethnocentric lenses.

Certainly he has a point when he compares what he sees in crowded, chaotic, polluted Bangkok, Guangzhou, or Manila to what he is used to. "The corruption is unbelievable, on a scale that can't be imagined. They've polluted their environment with abandon. I build hotels for them in which they want the waste to go directly into the rivers. The people on the top rip off everyone else, without regard for how it hurts their country."

When I pointed out to Kevin that through the eyes of a Thai, Korean, or Malay, his life seems just as corrupt, uncivilized, and incomprehensible, he responded angrily: "Then why do they all want to come here? And look at their educational system they are so proud of in Japan or Singapore or Hong Kong. They produce a nation of robots. Sure they do well academically but they have no ideas of their own. They aren't capable of original thought. By any standard you want to name, their schools ultimately fail them."

I rise to the challenge. "It depends on what outcome you are looking for. In a culture that values discipline and cooperation over independence, they are interested in a different product. They are amazed by the violence, the lack of discipline and dignity in our people. They—"

This debate, in all its various permutations, is really about letting go of judgments about other cultures, comparing them to our own. People sense the arrogance, the critical attitudes of tourists who make little attempt to go beneath the surface of their customs. Note, for example, how you shake your head in amusement at the ways things are done differently when you travel. You may even make fun of strange accents, ridicule foreign dress, and denigrate cultural practices that are different from your own. Note, also, the critical attitude you may adopt when foreign visitors engage in behaviors you find incomprehensible.

Dennison Nash is an anthropologist interested in how the ways people travel reflect their cultural roots. In comparing Japanese versus American tourists, for example, you can't help but notice that Japanese travel in larger groups. Often they are ridiculed for their behavior, as well as their tendency to remain insulated from the places they visit. Stereotypical views associate them with tour buses, expensive cameras, and shopping binges. Similarly, Westerners often remark derogatorily about Japanese tourists' inclinations to remain aloof, to stay only with their own kind.

But within the culture of Japan, travel means something different from what it means to North Americans. Kinship bonds, team spirit, and group-oriented structures permeate every facet of life. Furthermore, a Japanese tourist is not just traveling as an individual but as a representative of the home group. Ritualized farewell parties are given in which the traveler is showered with gifts, good luck charms, even money to spend. It is fully expected that these generous offerings will be reciprocated in kind upon return. So all the shopping and photograph sprees that you see Japanese tourists engaged in are not just for themselves but for all those left behind.

Once we understand this social context, we can see how each of us behaves according to the cultural norms that have been imposed on us. Each of us believes that our practices are better than anyone else's.

Even within North America, people of one region make fun of the cultural behavior indigenous to others. New Yorkers, Texans, Southern Californians, Québécois, or Georgians thus all have reputations for acting a particular way, usually portrayed in terms that are less than endearing.

The key for a true traveler is to see places you are visiting not on your own terms but by the standards of the native culture. There are good reasons why people act the ways they do. Kevin was unable—or more likely, unwilling—to consider that people who appeared uncivilized or unimaginative were acting appropriately within the norms of local expectations. One of the transformations that takes place when you examine other worlds outside of ethnocentric constraints is that you develop a greater degree of flexibility in looking at any situation from multiple viewpoints.

So the question remains: How do you form a mindset that keeps you open to new customs without needing to demean them? How do you travel in such a way that the process and people become more important than the place?

• *Do your homework.* Read about the cultural context of behavior that is typical for the region you are visiting.

• *Become aware of your judgments.* Monitor carefully the times when you are being critical of others. It happens so unconsciously and automatically that even the best of intentions are easily laid aside.

• *Practice empathy.* Walk inside other people's shoes (or sandals) and try to look out at the world through their eyes.

• *Be flexible.* Try out alternative ways of solving problems, especially those that are consistent with the local customs. Perhaps above all else, travel can help you resolve difficulties in more creative ways. This is especially the case when you make the point to be responsive and responsible in your interactions with people you meet.

TRAVELER'S RESPONSIBILITY

Travelers enjoy a special vantage point, as outsiders, from which to gain brief glimpses into other people's lives. We often see through the noise and distractions to the heart of the matter. Because we come from a different place and perspective, we are not just influenced by the people we visit—we influence them as well.

Being outsiders, we are able to bring fresh insights into the cultures we are visiting, especially if we offer them in a spirit that is respectful, loving, and nonjudgmental. One man relates, for example, an incident in which he accompanied a new friend he had met during a visit to his place of work. He was introduced to various colleagues of the friend and watched them in action. He then gave his somewhat innocent, fresh reactions to what he witnessed, observations that were considerably different from what had been expressed previously. It was this "foreign" perception that proved to be so helpful in clarifying some things that had been elusive. "Apparently," he explained further, "I noticed things that my friend had not seen and put them in a perspective that made some difference to him." He smiled apologetically, as if to say: "I don't mean to mess with things. I couldn't help myself. I just wanted to repay the kindness that had been extended to me."

There is a thrill of influencing others, leaving in your wake the remnants of good deeds that have helped others. In fact, most nights before I fall asleep, and every night I am on the road, I ask myself what I've done during that day that really matters.

It could have been a little thing really. Perhaps I brightened someone's life a bit by taking the time to say how much I appreciated their efforts on my behalf. Consistently, I try hard to be nice to people I meet, to give them the best of me, and thereby show my gratitude for their hospitality.

I believe that travelers have an obligation to be responsible—in the same sense that doctors take an oath to do no harm or that backpackers in wilderness areas leave nothing behind but their footprints and take nothing but photographs. Each of us is an ambassador for our tribe, whether that primary affiliation is based on nationality, ethnicity, local community, religion, or profession.

I recall skiing in Utah once, losing my ski in a snowdrift, and having three Mormon teenagers spend the better part of an hour helping me find it. I was stunned by their generosity and vowed that, ever after, I would repay gestures of kindness with efforts of my own. Since that time I remember dozens, perhaps hundreds, of similar incidents in which people have extended themselves to me with no expectation of reciprocity. I am paying them back by helping as many others as I can. Furthermore, another distinction I see between the tourist and traveler is that the former is steeped in selfness, in indulgence, while the latter gives as well as takes, returning as much or more—not in money but in kindness of spirit.

In the tradition of Jesus, Buddha, and Mohammed, the traveler's job is not just to enjoy life as it comes but to do good for others. There is no satisfaction quite like the rush of altruism, the "helper's high" that accompanies acts of good will.

I know that one purpose of travel for most of us is to escape, for just a little while, the obligation to take care of others that is so much a part of our lives. We are getting away in the first place to be selfish, to take care of ourselves, to experience maximum freedom in the acts of doing whatever we want whenever we want. Yet it does not detract from the pursuit of pleasure to also value helping and honoring others along the road. In the same way that boredom provides a context for excitement, so too does offering the best parts of ourselves to others make self-indulgence even more satisfying. The sorts of relationships that involve giving of ourselves to others, even during brief visits to their lives, also permits us to look deeper into the worlds we are passing through.

———

Transformative travel most often occurs through interactions with people. It is by asking questions, engaging in relationships with local inhabitants, that we are afforded opportunities to examine our own behavior and customs. We change in the process of solving problems in new ways, often with the assistance and support of new friends.

While this helpfulness is a significant part of making sure you don't return the same again, it isn't the only change agent. Just as important is the spirit of adventure and risk taking that leads you to venture into new territory.

8

If It's Adventure You Are After

$\mathcal{M}$ost trips do not lead to substantial change; their purpose is primarily for entertainment, business, or a well-deserved rest from the stresses of daily life. If you are really after personal growth, you will want to adopt a particular attitude and select a special perceptual filter that will allow you to see things, and yourself, a bit differently. This will only happen if you immerse yourself in the world you are visiting, not as a tourist but as an adventurer.

This is not as difficult as it sounds—once you enter any culture different from your own, you are confronted with a maze of situations that turn your world upside down. Every time you cross the road it is an adventure. People don't drive in orderly lanes, or they use roundabouts instead of stop signs, or the signs are in an unfamiliar language, or traffic comes from the opposite direction, and all of a sudden you feel completely lost. The stated prices of things don't reflect what they are actually sold for. It takes a major effort to figure out how to get from where you are to anywhere else. When you walk across the street, you aren't sure any longer which way to look. All your previous experience in familiar situations no longer helps you make good decisions.

What I am describing is a state of hypervigilence or super-alertness, in which all your senses are tuned up a few notches. You notice things you wouldn't otherwise. You discover all over again what it is like to learn to drive, or order from a menu, or purchase something you want. Your sense of smell picks up odors you never knew existed. You hear sounds that are unfamiliar, see things that have no place in your existing catalogue of images. You even feel things that have no definable label, think thoughts that don't make sense. This is what travel does to you. It takes away the walls, the floor, the ceiling of your perceptions.

In this chapter we examine the ways that adventure-based travel, whether as a planned enterprise or an event quite spontaneous, promotes lasting and meaningful changes in the ways you perceive and relate to the world.

THE INTREPID TRAVELER

If you are really honest, traveling is a tremendous pain. Long hours of boredom. Being scrunched into small places. Waiting in lines. Being lost in unfamiliar territory. Getting cheated and ripped off. Sleeping in strange beds with lumpy pillows. Upset stomachs. Rude people. Unexpected delays. Overpriced food. It costs a dollar just to make a phone call from a hotel room!

Like giving birth, you tend to forget the long wait and excruciating pain because you like the result. You may even try again, although many times thereafter you will have your moments of regret. Still, anything worth doing in life involves work and some degree of adventure. If you're after really rich rewards then you know you have a lot of sacrifices, inconveniences, and hard work ahead of you. This is no less true with travel.

If you are after luxury, convenience, and familiarity, stay home or go the tourist route. That's not to say that to be growthful travel must involve slogging through mud and mosquitoes. Rather, that to get to exotic locales, whether in the world or in your own mind and heart, you must often travel vast distances, or at least to remote areas without direct routes. This necessarily means a certain degree of annoyance and even pain.

I have mentioned previously that change does not come easy. You won't find it waiting in your first-class seat or hotel room but in those environments that challenge you the most, whether that is a market-place, jungle, or mountaintop.

Hierarchy of Travel Snobbery

Self-described adventure travelers ridicule tourists in their stereotypical wardrobes and behavior, snickering at their superficiality and timidity—the way they keep their arrogance intact while refusing to face the world without structures and guides. Yet anthropological travelers like Claude Levi-Strauss despise self-promoting adventure travelers just as much. In his mind, real travel—the kind that teaches you something profound—requires months of patience, boredom, and hardship before you stumble onto what you're looking for. Adventurers are, most of all, impatient: they want it all, and they want it now!

While both adventure and anthropological travelers ridicule tourists because of their tendency to collect useless souvenirs instead of stories that elicit pity and terror, Pico Iyer introduces still another category called *overlanders.* These are the true road warriors, the ones who practice a code of locomotion that prohibits either air transportation or air-conditioned buses. They are only at home riding on the backs of trucks on dusty roads, staying in backpacker lodges without baths or maid service. "Overlanders," writes Patricia Perkins, "aim at nothing except an exhaustive knowledge of suffering."

There is a reverse sort of snobbery operating here, a class struggle in which the have-nots are proud of their poverty and simplicity. They take pride in how little they need, how economically they transport themselves from place to place, and especially how few articles they carry in their backpacks. If tourists use matched luggage and travelers prefer internal frame backpacks, overlanders are fond of army surplus duffel bags—or better yet, extra-strength garbage bags.

Tourists, adventurers, anthropologists, overlanders—each group has a distinct style of movement with its own code of conduct. Yet adventurers and tourists are not as different as they think, at least for those who rely on structures to provide them with desired experiences. What is the difference, really, between someone who spends the day on a city bus tour versus another who goes scuba diving? Assuming it is not a first-time event for either one to ride a bus or dive, each is engaging in familiar experiences that are intended not so much to transform as to entertain. That it is supposed to take more energy and courage for one over the other is beside the point.

Personal changes do not necessarily result from adventure-based travel. In some ways, adventures can actually be used to avoid such changes. Take, as one example, the person who decides to spend a week on a "live aboard" dive boat in the Fijian islands. Sounds pretty exotic and adventurous, doesn't it? Conjures up images of someone who is physically fit, a risk taker, a person who will really grab life and hold on with both hands.

Indeed this diver will return with tangible evidence of the adventure—beautiful shells and coral, a T-shirt with the name of the boat, and a videotape of a swim among sharks.

Yet life on a "live aboard" can be as insulated as a trip on a tour bus. Such experiences, while immensely exhilarating, relaxing, and entertaining, are no more likely to produce lasting personal changes for some people than a week in a beach resort. This is not because these trips don't have potential transformative value, just that many people are not looking for that sort of experience.

A diver on this Fijian trip may not, apart from the brief visit to Nadi Airport, come into contact with any part of the culture or people of the country; the boat could have been cruising anywhere. Except for some of the crew members, everyone on board is probably North American, veterans of many such cruises. The days are carefully regimented and partitioned according to diving schedules. Even conversations among those aboard tend to follow a predictable course in which people talk mostly about places they have been diving before and where they intend to go next.

When they return from their adventures, they'll feel relaxed—satisfied and eager to plan for the next diving trip. Although personal changes can and do occur as a result of these excursions—from the magic of seeing sea creatures underwater and the intimate friendships that emerge from living in such close quarters—they are not really a part of the plan.

Something to Prove

To some degree, adventure is part of every memorable trip. It is a component of travel that, while exhilarating and probably necessary for personal change to take place, stirs feelings of ambivalence in us. Adventure, after all, often means doing without things. Whether it is boredom, escape, or sheer madness that drives us, more and more people are willing to do without showers, newspapers—even oxygen if you are scuba diving or mountain climbing. In writing about this back-to-nature adventure phenomenon—the most rapidly growing segment of the travel industry—Jerry Adler wonders what exactly the appeal is: "Nature has wild animals in it, which make for every American's worst nightmare: being eaten alive and discovering *there's nobody to sue.*"

On one hand, we hunger for new challenges that will test our resolve; on the other, we feel perfectly miserable when subjected to the usual hardships that accompany adventures. These ambivalent feelings are, in fact, the best indicators that we are smack in the middle of an adventure. It is when you say to yourself, as Thorton Wilder did in *The Matchmaker,* "Oh, now I've got myself into an awful mess; I wish I were sitting quietly at home." Of course, Wilder continues, you know you are *really* in trouble "when you sit quietly at home wishing you were out having lots of adventures."

Some people begin adventures, subjecting themselves to "awful messes," because they have something to prove, either to themselves or to others. That has been the case with a number of women explorers who wanted to show the world they were hardly the weaker sex. Aviator Amelia Earhart, for example, chose to fly the Atlantic alone for this reason: "It was, in a measure, a self-justification—a proving to me, and to anyone else interested, that a woman with adequate experience could do it."

An even more remarkable case of confronting personal challenges on an adventure, considering her stature (four feet, nine inches) and culture (Japanese), is Junko Tabei—the first woman to climb Mount Everest and the first of her gender to break the stranglehold men of her country have had on the practice of exploration. She had been scorned and ridiculed by other mountaineers, and forbidden to join their clubs. Still she persisted and was profoundly changed by her ascent of the world's highest peak. She lost her fear of speaking her mind afterward and was no longer willing to pretend she was weak. She also stopped caring what people said behind her back.

All of these personality changes took place as a result of her persistence in conquering not only a mountain but the prejudices of her own people. Now she is a hero in her own land, a model for other young women who aspire to pursue their own dreams. In the true fashion of a traveler who enjoys the journey as much as the goal, Tabei believes that "climbing the mountain is its own reward."

That may be true to some extent, but Tabei—and many others like her—search out progressively more dangerous challenges because they have something to prove. Why, after all, do people risk their lives to face physical and emotional challenges during travels? Why do they climb mountains, cross oceans, or—as in the case of Helen Thayer— walk to the North Pole?

At the age of fifty, Thayer willingly subjected herself to unstable ice pack, fierce storms, starvation, polar bears, and cold so biting that one of her greatest dangers was freezing her eyes shut permanently if she allowed herself to cry. Upon surviving her first encounter with three polar bears, Thayer was filled with pride and satisfaction. Though she had been sick with fear, she had stayed calm enough to do what must be done. Once you have faced such life-threatening circumstances in the Arctic, at fifty degrees below zero, completely alone, there is nothing you can't handle back home. That's exactly how Thayer described her feelings after chasing the bears away: "I passed my first test."

Why People Climb Mountains

The question of why people climb mountains and willingly subject themselves to other life-threatening situations is one that requires some analysis. Adventurers are deliberately risking their safety, even their lives, to travel to a particular spot with a view. Family and friends often wonder why mountaineers willingly hang from rock ledges by their fingernails while buffeted by high winds and blinding snowstorms. Among the reasons offered most frequently are: freedom, the rush, feelings of personal control, testing one's limits, pure joy in movement, feeling competent, focused engagement, aesthetic appreciation, and spiritual transcendence.

After coming within inches of dying in a rock climbing accident, Rob Schultheis found that something powerful and inexplicable happened to him during his recovery and descent down the mountain alone. Filled with joy at being alive and a sense of clarity that was at once startling and unnerving, he was able to do things he thought were impossible.

"Shattered, in shock, I climbed with the impeccable sureness of a snow leopard, a mountain goat. I crossed disintegrating chutes of rock, holds vanishing from under my hands and feet as I moved, a dance in which a single missed beat would have been fatal. . . . What I am doing is absolutely impossible, I thought. I can't be doing this. But I have the grace, the radiant mojo, and here I am!"

As a result of this adventure and life-threatening mishap, he became a person he no longer recognized: "The person I became on Neva was the best possible version of myself, the person I should have been throughout my life. No regrets, no hesitation; there were no false moves left in me."

Apparently, the stress-induced altered state that Schultheis experienced is not unusual among those who love adventure. Some people devote their lives to the pursuit of travel thrills that make them feel more alive. They push themselves to the edge of their own capabilities, braving danger, exhaustion, and risks so that they can move to a more intense level of being. They use extreme skiing, hunting, free climbing, distance running, and swimming as a means to attain the elusive state of physical and mental perfection where there is no room for hesitation or mistakes.

Unfortunately, by nightfall, Schultheis's revelation and resolution began to slip away. By then he remembered mostly that desperation and helplessness had driven him to new depths of his own potential. He had tasted heaven and now he was "stuck back on earth, with no sign of redemption." Was this a blessing or a curse?

One caution here: There is considerable evidence that one effect of placing yourself in the path of danger is that you produce a temporary biochemical high that becomes addictive. While this experience is often elicited during adventure activities, and especially extreme sports, it is most often temporarily uplifting rather than transformative. The impact doesn't last. The adventurer begins craving progressively more challenging situations to stimulate altered states of consciousness.

It's hardly necessary to place yourself in real danger to enjoy the benefits of adventure-based travel activities. As long as you find a challenge that forces you to move beyond your present levels of competence, there is likely to be some personal reward from the experience.

Indeed, increased skill at problem solving is a likely result of adventure-based activities like mountain climbing. Often what has been learned on a rock face can be generalized to other aspects of life as well. Mountaineer James Ullman describes, for example, how an accomplished climber must learn to overcome the tendency to move in stuttering steps up a mountain, finding a foothold, resting there awhile before moving up to the next level. Equilibrium and balance are attained by maintaining a continuous rhythm, just as skaters or bicyclists would fall if they were to stop after each movement. It is continuous motion that allows a climber to maintain balance, even in the face of circumstances in which a tiny fingerhold is all that a mountain offers. "The result is that by constant rhythmic movement and the ingenious use of friction, an accomplished cragsman can often master short stretches of vertical or near-vertical rock which would be insurmountable by the ordinary methods of 'stop and go.'"

If you learn this concept of balance through motion on a mountain you can apply it with equal fluidity in other areas of life. This is when a recreational experience becomes a transformative one.

PLANNED ADVENTURES

One of the fastest-growing segments of the travel industry is the operation of learning vacations designed to educate people about the world or themselves. One such structured program, No Limits, prides itself on pushing participants beyond their own perceived capabilities. Mary Cain, one mountain climbing instructor for the program, explains to her charges: "I want the experience to be right at the edge of what you're capable. It doesn't have to do with your guide's edge, or your buddy's edge. It's only going to be an experience when it's your edge."

Enterprising businesspeople well understand the appeal that the *perception* of danger holds for those on vacation. It isn't necessary for an activity to be risky as long as people believe it is so.

Take bungy jumping, for instance. More people are injured crossing the road to sign up for this supposedly reckless sport than actually jumping off its 150-foot tower while attached to its rubber rope. A. J. Hackett, the company that runs most of these concessions around the world, proclaims in its brochure: "Suddenly something you thought was impossible, becomes possible. You will come away from one of our unique sites with a memory that will be with you forever. Remember that you did something that you didn't believe you could do—so use this experience in other areas of your life." Good advertising. Even better psychology. The company isn't far wrong in its grasp of which elements lead to internal changes:

- *Programmed expectations.* If a therapist, teacher, or adventure outfitter says that what you are about to experience is really going to make a big difference in your life—*and you believe it*— more often than not, personal change will result.

- *Illusions of danger.* By definition, an adventure must *appear* to be risky. Otherwise, surviving the ordeal doesn't seem like much of an accomplishment.

- *Indelible memories.* The object of vacation experiences is create images that you will not soon forget. Essentially, you are paying to wire your brain with particular memories.

- *Overcoming fear.* Ideally, the best adventures are those in which you were reluctant to participate but went through with it anyway. You conquered your fears.

- *Public witnesses.* When people are watching, it is harder for you to back down during moments of doubt. You also have sources of support before and after the experience, as well as comrades to talk to afterward.

Whether we are talking about jumping off a tower or out of a plane, riding a roller coaster or a speedboat, the object of any canned adventure is to get your heart beating quickly, to jolt you with an electric shock of awareness that you are alive. The possibility that you could be injured, or even killed, is often what makes the adventure appealing.

Motels in tourist areas provide information on a wide range of these adventure activities. In one such establishment, I observed a whole section of brochures devoted to thrill seeking—not only bungy jumping but whitewater rafting, blackwater rafting (in a cave), rappelling, wilderness hiking, mountain biking, sky diving, hang gliding, hot air ballooning, rock climbing, jet skiing, scuba diving, snorkeling, parasailing, hunting, horseback riding, wildlife viewing, and deep sea fishing. The same rack offered helicopter flights, four-wheel drive safaris, and X-rated adventures (whatever *that* entails).

So we feed our hunger for excitement in controlled doses, especially when on vacation. You willingly pay hefty sums for things you would ordinarily never do. You know you'll come back alive without a scratch on you—these folks have liability to worry about. They'll take care of your safety, all the while they expose you to things that have been proven again and again to get the blood flowing.

Am I saying that going on canned adventures really isn't any different from visiting museums or shopping? In some ways, yes. The results *are* predictable and consistently satisfying. Canned adventures *do* provide a structure for you to try new experiences when you return to your other life. If it's out of character for you to jump off a cliff or out of an airplane, and you like the way it feels when you try it, you may become more inventive in bed, in your social interactions, or on the job. The key is whether your mindset is tuned toward distraction, entertainment, or growth.

It's not an either-or proposition. You can have fun *and* learn something about yourself. Canned adventures do indeed produce reliable results in measured amounts. What they lack in spontaneity and unpredictability they make up for in convenience and safety. You know exactly what you will get, money back guaranteed.

UNEXPECTED ADVENTURES

When her whole family decided to spend the day on an outing to visit one of the longest roller coasters in the world, Miriam decided to pass. It wasn't because of lack of interest: she liked roller coasters and also the prospect of sharing fun with her family. She decided, however, to try something else. She resisted the impulse to stay by the pool and read a good novel, or to shop for clothes. She asked herself instead what would be hardest for her to do, what would be most challenging.

When she went through the list of possibilities, the one option she skirted over most quickly involved approaching people to engage them on a personal level. She had reason for her apprehension. She certainly didn't want her behavior misconstrued, and in these dangerous times, she also didn't want to meet up with some crazy person who might hurt her. She had visions of being raped, kidnapped, or robbed. She also wondered how she would approach people in a way they would respond cordially.

Miriam settled on a museum as a likely place to talk to people, and yet feel safe doing so. She also decided that she wouldn't plan very much what would happen, another departure from her usual routines. She'd just try to remain open, to focus not so much on the things in the museum as the people. Furthermore, she resolved to engage people on a deeper level than she would normally. She would try to find out what was important to them.

Several hours later, her family returned to the room to find her sitting on the balcony, deep in thought. They were positively excited, the adrenaline rush still flowing through their veins.

"Mom," her youngest child immediately jumped in. "Guess what? I went on the ride *four* times and one time I didn't even hold on at all even though I was scared and Lisa was pushing me and trying to scare me even more—"

"So, how was your day?" her husband interrupted, puzzled by her pensive look.

"Fine. I guess," she replied, not at all sure what her day was like. "I didn't have anything particular in mind. Just to meet people and talk to them. . . . Yeah, yeah, I know. That's so unlike me. That's why I wanted to do it. I've been on roller coasters before and I know what that's like. But I don't know what it's like to be more . . . I don't know . . . more. . . ."

Her thoughts trailed away as she considered what exactly she *had* been searching for. The day had not gone at all as she had expected. She did approach several people, mothers and children most of all, and she did talk to them. But the encounters remained shallow and unsatisfying. Maybe she'd been expecting too much during a first, experimental foray. She realized other people didn't share much because she hadn't revealed much of herself.

"Next time," she heard herself say to her husband. And there *would* be a next time. There was so much she felt confused about but one thing she knew for certain—if she continued to push herself to do what was most challenging rather than comfortable she would improve her skills and personal resources. Realistically, the only goal of this first excursion had been to do it, not to do it well. That would come with practice.

—⁓—

If it is really adventure you are after, then it isn't necessary to trek the Himalayas or raft the Colorado River; it is possible to create adventures out of almost any setting as long as you force yourself to do what you are most avoiding. You must also be prepared to face unexpected setbacks: it is inevitable that at some point your trip will take an expected turn in a direction that you would neither choose or even desire.

9

When Things Go Wrong

In spite of your best plans and most meticulous preparation, it's inevitable that things will not unfold as you had anticipated. This not only reflects the common run of fortune but also presents the best opportunities for personal growth and change. After all, it is dealing with the unexpected that shakes you up, that stirs up internal conflict to the point where significant learning takes place. Although this condition of novelty and disorientation can test you in ways you would have preferred to avoid, the most miserable experiences tend to compose the most entertaining stories after you get back.

HOW COULD THIS BE HAPPENING TO ME?

Novelist Michael Dorris recounts an amazing journey from Princeton, New Jersey, to Anchorage, Alaska, by a somewhat circuitous route. He first got the bright idea that he might save some money—as well as see some sights along the way—if he flew via Japan Airlines, which routed their flights through London. Just before his plane was to land,

Heathrow closed down because of fog. The pilot continued on to Paris, also closed because of a snowstorm. He tried Rome next—also closed—so he headed to Frankfurt. After changing planes, the passengers tried Rome again, only to be turned back. Dorris lived through three more false starts before he finally made it to his destination.

You're not impressed. I can tell. You have your own stories. You ended up on one end of the planet, your bags on the other end. Or the plane's wing caught fire. Or perhaps you spent two days in residence at O'Hare Airport waiting for the weather to clear.

These stories are not only hardly unusual but depressingly familiar. For thousands of years travelers have been complaining about similar glitches—about rented yaks that proved notoriously stubborn at the crucial moment of crossing the Khyber Pass, or hired guides who turned out to be bandits in disguise. If you don't die or become permanently disfigured from these adventures, your stories are golden.

I've written whole books that began with a single glitch in my travel plans. *On Being a Therapist,* the story of how therapists deal with the stresses and strains of their work, grew out of a frightening expedition into the Peruvian Amazon investigating the healing practices of witch doctors. *Growing a Therapist* was born during an unexpected rainstorm when I was trapped in a narrow canyon waiting for a flash flood to overtake me. *The Language of Tears* was first conceived as I was recovering from a near-death experience, thawing out from hypothermia in the New Zealand bush.

The disasters that befall us, however terrifying and excruciatingly painful at the time, seem comical in retrospect. They almost seem worth the aggravation for the pure entertainment value of the stories we get to tell.

Mary Mackey, for example, tells of a visit to Costa Rica in which her whole hotel was invaded by army ants that devoured everything in their path. Somehow, the hotel staff had mysteriously disappeared during the night, leaving the guests to fend for themselves. Then to make matters worse (yes, worse!), scorpions began falling from the ceiling like hail, dozens at a time, trying to save their own thick skins from invading ant hordes. "We rose like one person, fled back to our rooms, seized our umbrellas, opened them to keep off the scorpions, and retreated to the lobby, where we sat, hunched up against one another, like people waiting for a bus."

Stop chuckling. It's not *that* funny. Especially if you were there at the time. But these make such marvelous stories, don't they? Unfortunately, that seems like small consolation at the time. It is the collection of stories, however, that pushes us to enter such dubious circumstances where our sanity will later be called into question. "Tell me again," your mother will ask, "*why* you went there in the first place."

Surviving Trials and Tribulations

Traveling is certainly dangerous. From the first moment you arrive at an airport, you hear announcements warning you that people will try to sneak bombs into your luggage if you leave it unattended. Then the guards do a standard weapons check of all passengers, trying to catch those carrying knives, guns, and other implements of destruction. You can buy life insurance at this point.

Upon boarding the flight, the first thing they do is tell you what to do if the plane should lose altitude, lose control, or crash. It is something less than reassuring to be told that if you should fall into the water, your seat cushion will float.

As often as not, adventures go bad. They are, by their very nature, unpredictable forays into the unknown. You may hope that a particularly adventurous trip will be transformative, but you don't know exactly *how* it will change you, for better or for worse.

People ask us upon our return from an adventure what it was like and we lie through our teeth, or at least gloss over a few significant details. After coming back from a trek to the top of a dormant volcano in New Zealand, I had beautiful photos to show my family and friends. Indeed the views were spectacular and the trip itself was exotic and unique. Except for two companions, one of whom was a forest ranger in the area, nobody had ever ventured up this route before. I positively glowed as I told the story of our arduous climb and the satisfaction I felt making it to the top and back in one piece.

What I left out was that this was one of the worst days of my life. Our guide had no idea where we were most of the time. He had assured us it would be just a few hours to the top, so we brought with us only a little water and no food. There was no trail to follow, and we walked through dense forest, vines tangling our feet, sharp branches abrading our legs—all up a steep slope. Then it got a *lot* worse. At points the bush was so thick and impenetrable we had to get on our hands and knees and crawl. Then it got worse still: there was no choice but to slither on our bellies through mud and prickly bushes that lacerated our backs and arms. This went on for hours and hours until we reached the summit. Then it was a long journey back, lost most of the way.

After I showered and fed myself, reasonably recovered even though I looked like I had been tortured, I cheerfully wrote in my journal: "That's the thing about adventures: you just never know what's going to happen."

Actually, one thing you know for certain is that something about an adventure will go bad or it doesn't really count as a legitimate quest. Tony Wheeler, a writer for the *Lonely Planet Guides,* claims that real travelers love things to go wrong. Why else, he asks, would anyone go to India or Peru in the first place—except for dysentery? The only question is whether it will be bacillary or amoebic.

Since there is no way to avoid disagreeable encounters, the only variable is the degree of grace you face them with. Over the course of forty years on the road, Jan Morris has visited every major city on Earth. No matter how unpleasant the conditions, how rude the people, or how many things go wrong, she has been determined to avoid self-pity, to make the best of any situation. "The most ghastly cities have unavailingly tried to depress me, the vilest bureaucracy has not been able to expunge the ingratiating leer from my face. I can outsmile them all."

What a remarkable feat that is indeed! Yet this single attribute, more than any other, is what helps a traveler recover quickly from anything unforeseen or unpleasant. An inattentive waiter? A stolen wallet? A canceled flight? A room with paper-thin walls? A bed with spiders? Mere annoyances. Minor inconveniences. Hardly worth mentioning before you do whatever needs to be done to make things right.

In a collection of essays by writers on the terrible experiences they've suffered while traveling—caught in a border town when a war broke out or dodging sexual predators in Egypt—Jan Morris wonders why so many of her colleagues encounter such bad luck and misadventures while she seems immune. Upon reflection, she concludes that because she expects the best, she gets the best: "Being of sanguine temperament myself I have so far found in life, as in travel, that the worst seldom comes about."

I think that a more likely explanation is that bad things *do* happen to her as often as to any other traveler; the difference is in the way she casually shrugs off things that don't go as anticipated. She expects the best in people, and even when disappointed, does not dwell over matters. She prefers to look at the best in any situation.

Taking this attitude one step further, pains and annoyances are not necessarily to be avoided but embraced. The goal is not to remain comfortable but rather to feel everything more intensely. The object of travel for many great writers, from Mark Twain and Graham

Greene to Paul Theroux, is to get yourself in trouble so you have something to write about. Robert Louis Stevenson loved to travel for this very reason: "The great affair is to move; to feel the needs and hitches of our life more nearly; to come down off this feather-bed of civilization, and find the globe granite underfoot and strewn with cutting flints."

Just as in therapy or self-help books, people want easy cures. They don't want to have to work for their personal changes. They want them handed on a platter. They want pills to change their moods. They want tricks and techniques that will provide instant relief. They want to pay surrogates to suffer on their behalf. They want discounts and shortcuts so they can enjoy the benefits of self-discovery without paying full price. Unfortunately, the only way that you can learn to find your way is to get yourself lost.

Being Lost

One condition that you absolutely must master is the feeling of being lost. If you travel correctly, becoming lost is not only inevitable but desirable; this is when your adventures really begin. In spite of all your preparation, and all the resources you have at your disposal, you will most certainly end up in places that were not on your itinerary, nor even on your map. The crucial test is how you deal with this predicament.

First of all, you must accept the premise that becoming lost is not altogether an unfortunate circumstance. Unlike at home when getting lost means you will be late for somewhere you need to be, during travel the only place you are supposed to be is where you already are. Also, whereas being lost on your own turf is a sign of ignorance, incompetence, or perhaps neglect, there is an honor associated with being lost as a traveler. After all, this is the first time you have ever explored this territory.

Another crucial aspect of dealing with being lost is asking for directions, a challenge that is especially trying if the natives speak another language. Robert Packard advises that whatever else you do, don't ever bring out a map—most people find them so bewildering they become paralyzed or incoherent. "The fascination of such people locating their own geographic whereabouts (the very spot you don't want to be) transcends their possible help in guiding you elsewhere."

Packard recommends further that you present yourself to prospective direction-givers as trustworthy, humble, despairing, and not too bright (this is easy because that's exactly how you feel). It is now extremely important to remember that wherever you are being sent off to may as likely lead you further astray as closer to your desired destination.

Even though I routinely check directions with not just two but *three* independent sources, I still end up far in the opposite direction from where I thought I wanted to be. It is at this point that I give up my search for the restaurant, museum, or mountain I was looking for and instead decide to discover, if not appreciate, wherever I am. I really have no choice in the matter as I am a hopeless navigator. When I go hiking, I always get lost, although somehow I find my way back.

I once decided to take a course in compass and map reading. I couldn't control my excitement once I was introduced to my instructors, two master sergeants from the Desert Warfare School at Nellis Air Force Base. I bought topographical maps of the whole area. I invested in an expensive compass as well. We worked hard and I studied my lessons well. I even learned how to call in the coordinates for a bombing raid, accurate within three meters of any spot I chose.

That weekend, I ventured out into the mountains, my step quickened with anticipation and confidence. I stopped every few minutes to check compass readings and compare the topography to my trusty map, leading me to the peak I had set my sights on. I climbed steadily throughout the day until, finally, I had attained my goal. As I sat on my perch eating a snack, reveling in my prowess as the consummate tracker, I decided to check a few coordinates. I pulled out my map and discovered to my horror that although I had indeed climbed to the top of a mountain, it was definitely not the mountain I had wanted to climb. I learned then that not only was I hopeless, but that I had better get used to it.

Among all the worst travel stories I ever heard, the most interesting, if not the most amusing, is the case of a woman traveling with her husband by train in Europe.

During the middle of the night, she awoke disoriented because she no longer heard the accustomed train sounds she had grown used to. She decided to investigate, as well as empty her bladder at the same time, so she put on her robe and wandered down the hall. She was surprised to discover that sometime during the night the train had been loaded onto a ferry to transport them across a body of water, the name of which eluded her since she couldn't even recall which countries she was passing through. She got off the train and walked around the ship a bit, trying to find a vacant bathroom. This proved to be more difficult than she imagined, because some festival or party was going on and the inebriated guests were sorely in need of all the facilities available.

Eventually, she found a vacant toilet, and just in time! On her way back to the train, she lost her way, uncertain even which deck level the train was parked. It couldn't have been more than a few minutes but felt like an hour before she located the appropriate place—now she recognized the train tracks on the floor. Unfortunately, however, there was no train in sight!

This was indeed a mystery. Wherever could they hide a train on a moving ship? It was at that moment she realized the ferry was no longer moving and that, somehow, while she was gone, the train continued its journey all the while her husband slept peacefully in their compartment.

She was on the edge of full-scale panic. Here she was stuck in her nightgown and a robe on a ship god-knows-where. Her train was gone. She had no passport, no money, no inkling even of where she was. I assure you that the last thing on her mind at that moment was what a great story this would make if and when she ever found her way home again.

She swallowed hard and took a deep breath. Then she wandered off the ferry to find herself among several other trains, one of which was pointed more or less in the direction she thought she should be heading. With little else to lose, unable even to explain to others in their language why she was dressed so strangely, she boarded the train and hoped for the best.

Obviously, the woman did some day return home—or I wouldn't have heard her tale. At the very first stop, before a conductor even had a chance to check the ticket she didn't have, she looked across the tracks and located what she thought-hoped-prayed might be her own train. She flew across the tracks and boarded it just as it began to leave. To her relief, she walked down the narrow corridor and recognized her berth. Her husband was still sound asleep, unaware that she had ever been gone.

It was some small consolation that she had such a delightful story to tell. Yet as travel writer Pico Iyer has observed repeatedly in his own tales: "The one great glory of traveling is always redeemed by commotion recollected in tranquility."

If she were honest, this woman would admit (she didn't) that her hour of sheer terror was worth the lifetime of mileage she got out of retelling the tale over and over again. Yet it was *because she was lost* that the whole journey became memorable; otherwise, she would have no recollection whatsoever of this night in her life.

I am not advocating that we should try to get lost more (although it's probably not a bad idea), merely that when we do lose our way that we see the situation as much as an opportunity as a disaster. This is what separates the timid tourists from the adventurous travelers: the former make every effort to ensure that nothing ever does go wrong; the latter recognize that it is only unfamiliar situations that force them to adapt rather quickly to new behavioral patterns.

THE CHALLENGES YOU WILL FACE

You can prepare yourself mentally by looking inward, or you can also consider what you are likely to encounter on the outside, as part of your immersion in the culture of a different place. In the literature on reentry for people planning to relocate to other places, there is an assumption that you have a much better chance of adjusting, if not flourishing, when you know what to expect and what challenges you will face. Preparation is thus a critical part of intelligent travel, especially those efforts directed toward planning for situations that will test you the most.

When Richard Brislin and several other cross-cultural scholars analyzed a hundred critical incidents that took place among people traveling abroad for extended periods, they wished to identify what the most frequent concerns were and how they were resolved most satisfactorily. If, for example, you were about to visit a strange land, wouldn't you want to know what people struggle with the most in their adjustments? Whether a diplomat, Peace Corps volunteer, technical advisor, soldier, foreign student, or business traveler, people have the same problems adjusting to life outside their own cultures. Among the most frequent challenges they face are the following.

Falling on Your Face

Whatever you might be used to doing in the way of social etiquette, table manners, or business policies would be considered uncivilized, backward, and ignorant in many other parts of the world. Many of the ways you routinely act now are just plain wrong in other places.

Try helping yourself to a dish at a Chinese banquet before you serve your neighbors and you will be considered selfish and ill mannered. Try allowing fellow motorists to cut in front of you while driving in

New York and you will be instantly recognized as a Midwestern hick. Try going to dinner at someone's home in a dry county in Alabama without bringing a bottle of Jack Daniels and you will be regarded as a heathen, a Yankee, or worse.

Putting Your Foot in Your Mouth

Don't delude yourself into thinking that Japanese, Mississippi, or Russian hosts can't feel your disdain for their cultures. They know it just as you know it when visitors from outside merely indulge your favorite haunts and pastimes.

You will never, ever be accepted by others as long as they can feel your critical judgment of their customs. The object is not to become more skilled at hiding your revulsion at public spitting, your disrespect at limp handshakes, your horror of beggars in the street, or your bemusement over customs you find quaint. Rather, the goal is to reach a point where you stop judging other practices by the standards of what is most familiar. The true test is when you can face novel situations with an open mind, with a willingness to consider other ways as being equal if not superior to your own.

Offending the Natives

Because you are likely to make lots of mistakes, you will offend people. Constantly. And never know why. It makes it difficult to adjust and correct your behavior when you don't process accurate feedback. There will be lots of situations when you notice that other people are reacting to you strangely. Rather than assuming that their reactions mean there is something wrong with them, try assuming that it is far more likely that you have acted in some insensitive way. Find out what you did so you don't repeat your mistakes.

Stressing Out

The stress from facing constant challenges is accumulative. People do things differently in various parts of the world. It is exhausting learning new customs for how to shop, communicate, or take care of your most basic needs. This isn't the case just with visiting a foreign country but in every region of our own continent.

In addition to stressing out over differences, you must also contend with other things going wrong such as lost reservations or baggage. Like so many of these challenges, you can think of them as disasters or opportunities for growth.

One woman recalls with a smile:

> The best trip I ever had in my life was a trip my family took to Yellowstone National Park. Our Jeep was packed full with bodies and baggage, including a large container full of clothes and sleeping bags mounted on the roof rack. The first day, somehow our sleeping bags blew off the roof. The second day we managed to lose everything remaining on top. Here we were on our way to a camping trip without any clothes or sleeping bags!
>
> What surprised me was that we found our situation hilarious. Laughing together over this "disaster" actually brought us together in a way that couldn't have happened otherwise. Ordinarily, back at home, I would have found this so stressful I couldn't have enjoyed myself at all. This time, though, we supported one another and dealt with the situation as best we could. There is nothing we ever did as a family that created such learning and intimacy.

Losing Your Voice

You have a specialized vocabulary and style of communication that works best in your own home, and to a lesser extent, in your city, state, and region of the country. After that, your fluency diminishes rapidly in direct proportion to distance traveled.

Try making yourself understood in rural Louisiana, or Boston, or parts of San Francisco, San Antonio, or Chicago. Your vocabulary becomes limited. You rely more on gestures, less on words. And as you venture to other countries where people speak altogether different languages, you try to get by with the verbal fluency of a three-year-old: "water," "toilet," "Pepto Bismol."

Pain and Suffering

The harder it is to get to a place, the more you appreciate the destination upon arrival. There is, therefore, a noble suffering common to the transformative traveler. There is also an acceptance of pain and inconvenience, as if this is part of the normal course of events.

In one of the side canyons of the Grand Canyon lies a magical world of waterfalls located on the Havasupai Reservation. The Indian residents have developed progressively more comfortable lodging for tourists over the years. Not too long ago, there were only two ways to get to this place. The first option was a five-day rafting trip down the Colorado River followed by a ten-mile round-trip hike along a rough trail to visit the falls and swim in the pools. The second alternative was to backpack twenty miles, round-trip, into the canyon carrying enough supplies to last a week. In both cases, the journey to this secluded spot involved quite a lot of sweat, blisters, and a sizable commitment of time and energy.

To sit in one of the perfect pools and soak your aching body as you view the cascades of the Supai Falls has to be one of the most satisfying pleasures of life. You feel proud of what it took to get to this sacred spot. You savor every moment of the view—and your bath—as you realize how much you sacrificed to indulge in this pleasure. Even as you scale the sheer switchbacks on your way out, staggering under the weight of your pack, you pause from your grim death march to relive the swim under the falls.

When the Havasupai Indians began helicopter service to the bottom of the canyon and built a luxury hotel to house those tourists who like their conveniences, the falls became accessible to a wider audience. Indeed, if you look at people sitting in the water you can't easily tell which ones walked in under their own power and which ones dropped in out of the sky. I would submit, however, that although their photographs of the falls may look identical, the two groups' sensations in the water are not.

You get exactly what you are willing to pay for—in life or in travels. If what you want to pay for is luxury and convenience, that is what you will get. If, on the other hand, you are willing to invest some time, energy, hard work, commitment, and considerable planning, you will create an altogether different sort of journey.

Of course, roughing it isn't always associated with constructive change. We all enjoy tastes of indulgence; we all like to be pampered on occasion. In fact, during the reflective stage when you are looking back on what you experienced, there is nothing like a hot shower, a clean bed, and room service to help you appreciate where you have just been.

Keep in mind that convenience is associated with predictability, control, insulation, and efficiency. These are not exactly the variables that lead to growth. While they don't preclude opportunities for personal change, they do make them more difficult to achieve.

SOLVING PROBLEMS

I was attending a conference in Singapore, a city I imagined was pretty much like any other I'd been to. When I checked into the hotel with my assigned roommate, we were issued one key to the room. I politely asked for another one as well, figuring we would be going our separate ways at times and would need our own keys. The clerk explained politely that wouldn't be possible; they only have one key per room.

Ridiculous, I thought, and told him so. I'd never heard of such a thing. He politely but firmly insisted that each room had one key. I demanded to see the manager, who promptly repeated that one key was all they had. I then became quite indignant and made a scene, even though I knew I was missing something in this interaction. I just didn't know what it was.

My roommate and I continued up to our room with me still fuming. We moved our bags in and then proceeded to turn on the lights, none of which seemed to work. I returned to the desk and demanded another room, a request they immediately honored. We moved a few doors away but again we couldn't get the lights to work, or the air conditioning. I was livid by this time, ready to head home. My roommate, however, decided we should get someone up to help us: surely we were missing something.

Sure enough, the porter took our key and inserted it in a holder by the door, activating all the electricity in the room. It seems this system is common throughout Asia as a way to save electricity when nobody is in the room. Only one key is needed since it is always left at the desk on the way out.

I realized then what a fool I'd been. I applied the customs I was used to in a culture where they didn't fit. I responded out of ignorance. I just assumed these people were clowns, that the whole damn hotel was broken. One thing I refused to consider was that I was out of line. Ever since then, when I'm faced with a situation that isn't going the way I want, I now stop to think about what I might be missing, or what I don't know.

We are all enculturated to solve problems in particular ways based on principles that are familiar. So often travel experiences present us with situations in which our usual forms of tackling challenges no longer work. In the example just described, I was frustrated and confused primarily because I failed to ask the right questions. If I had let go of my assumptions about the ways freedom of movement in hotels is managed through keys, I might have simply said to the clerk: "I wonder how you handle things when two occupants leave the room at different times." He would have then explained how keys are left at the desk on the way out, and probably gone on to tell me about the slots in each room that activate power. Since I didn't ask the right questions, I wasn't able to figure out how to solve the problem.

The Stresses of Cultural Immersion

Thus far we have been speaking about travel as a romantic adventure, yet there are few challenges in life that are more stressful. There is a good reason why most people prefer their tour buses and museums over true immersion in another culture. For those who are trying to learn the language and customs of their temporarily adopted culture, headaches are common.

There are several characteristics of people who are likely to be successful in their adaption to life in another culture:

• *Transformative travelers think in terms of flourishing, growing, and thriving.* Their expectations for themselves lead them to create their happiness rather than wait for it to happen.

Nigel is a visiting teacher from Australia who is spending his summer break (our winter) learning about education in North America. He had decided he didn't want to be a mere tourist, that he really wanted to get a taste for what life is like for teachers in this culture. An admirable goal but hardly easy for him to implement.

Before long, Nigel felt homesick and lonely. He missed his family and friends. He found that once the novelty of his accent wore off, people tended to forget that he was a stranger in a strange land; increasingly, he spent more and more time alone. Finally, he decided he didn't like the way things were progressing and began to initiate more activities on his own. Rather than waiting for others to invite him to do things, he started reaching out to others. At about the time he was preparing to return home, even he didn't notice the difference in accents any longer.

• *Successful transformative travelers have a balanced support system of friends to help them bridge the cultural gaps.* Isolation, either alone or with others who have similar fears of mixing in, will only magnify feelings of alienation about "us" against "them." Those who make an effort to cultivate relationships with "natives," who attempt to learn the language and culture, who immerse themselves in the culture rather than criticize it, will necessarily feel more at home.

Cynthia spent a two-week vacation in Northern California. While I don't mean to imply that this region is a foreign culture, it does have its own unique set of customs, expectations for behavior, even a special vocabulary.

At first, Cynthia acted very much like a tourist—she went to Fisherman's Wharf and the Golden Gate Bridge, to the Monterey Aquarium and the Wine Country. All her time that first week was spent either in the company of a few friends she was visiting or on her own.

She couldn't believe how critical and cynical she was about the culture she was observing. What she was really feeling was defensive and disoriented because the norms for behavior seemed so different from what she was used to. People dressed differently. They talked differently. They spent their leisure time doing things that she found puzzling.

In her head, she made fun of the people a lot, ridiculed their priorities all the while she gaped at the magnificent scenery. With a few days left, she realized that whereas she had "done" all the sights, she didn't really know much about the cultures she had been observing as an outsider. Furthermore, she felt a hunger that somehow this trip could help her make some needed changes in her life.

It was quite atypical of her to initiate conversations with perfect strangers but she made herself do so in circumstances that felt safe. She cut off ties with her friends and spent all her time talking to as many people as she could. In Chinatown, she stopped looking at buildings and started talking to people. A whole afternoon vanished as she chatted with the owners of a restaurant hidden in a back alley. The evening's adventure was spent in a gay bar. Before long she was no longer critical of behavior she found threatening; much to her amazement, she had joined *them*.

The rest of that week fled all too quickly. As she reflected on her "field notes," Cynthia realized she had actually had two trips, the first week as a tourist who observed things from afar, the second week as a participant whose attitudes were now altered irrevocably.

• *Attitude plays a big part.* We all have a choice in how we wish to react to things happening around us. A mob scene at a public gathering can be comical or a disgusting mess; downtown traffic can be a game or a trial; having one's purse stolen can be inconvenient or a disaster. In each case, an attitude of flexibility, openness, acceptance of the inevitable will lead to greater satisfaction. While we can't change what is happening, or how others react, we can program ourselves to respond in favorable or unfavorable ways.

Kenneth had been warned repeatedly about the traffic in Bangkok. He was only stopping there for a few days before he continued onward to an island vacation. If truth be told, there was nothing he hated worse than congestion and chaos in a big city. That is why he chose to live and work in a small town.

Kenneth asked himself what he wanted from his upcoming travels. If it was just a brief and relaxing break in his otherwise predictable life, he told himself he would be better off staying at a hotel at the airport and moving on to his final destination as soon as he could. But what *was* his final destination, he asked himself?

Maybe, just maybe, he could help himself conquer a lifelong aversion toward congested cities. More than that, perhaps he could even help himself rethink what these strange, confusing cultures are all about.

His family wanted no part of this weird experiment. They were anxious to get to the crystal-clear water as soon as possible. His wife was looking forward to reading a bunch of novels that, because of her busy schedule as an attorney, she never had time to read. His teenage children had their own agendas to meet others of their age at the resort where they would be staying. So if Kenneth wanted to challenge himself, he would be doing so on his own.

Against his better judgment, he negotiated a few days away from his family and booked himself a room smack in the middle of one of the most chaotic cities on Earth. The second hour of the drive from the airport had his blood pressure pulsing out of control. He had a headache from all the honking. His eyes hurt from all the car fumes. He was drenched in sweat. And the taxi driver—the guy was crazy.

As a distraction, he tried to engage the driver in conversation. How can you *stand* this every day? The man looked at him over his shoulder, and then shrugged, as if to say what is the big deal; this is the way it is. That was only the first lesson in attitude adjustment that was to take place during the ensuing days.

Kenneth couldn't claim to his family that he had a good time. After all, he explained, this was only the first time in his life that he ever tried something like this. He was determined, however, to pursue this experiment further. In fact, the very next chance he got he was going to hone his city skills in New York. What really surprised him, though, was when he was back at work and his friends asked him about his vacation, he found himself talking more about the few days he spent in the big city than all the rest of the time he spent at the beach.

- *It's important to let go of things that don't work anymore.* As Westerners, we have certain strong preferences about the way things should work. We like efficiency above all else. Yet in other cultures, there is far more of an appreciation for the process of life rather than its goals.

The most frustrating thing that I have struggled with trying to immerse myself in Latin culture is the way that time is treated so differently. I am always on time, even a few minutes early. I am punctual to a fault. I think this is a wonderful trait, not only for me, but for everyone else in the world.

If I have learned one important lesson from cultures in South America, something I will try and retain always, it is an appreciation for the beauty rather than the ugliness of a slower, disorganized, but wonderfully stimulating life. There is enough ambition and striving in this world. Yes, perhaps the one thing that helps the most to appreciate life in another culture is to look around you with both eyes open. As you move from one place to another in your life, remember that the ride *is* more important than the destination.

Phases of Adjustment

Whether you immerse yourself in another culture for a brief visit or a more permanent stay, there is a predicable adjustment process that takes place. It helps to know what you might expect along this path so that you can prepare yourself for the bumps along the road.

During the *Entry Phase*, everything is new and exciting. You are enamored with differences in food, customs, rituals, and behavior. You can't get enough stimulation and feel drunk with the possibilities that open around you. All the richness and strangeness of your new environment stimulates you to the point where you feel fatigued—overwrought and yet exhausted.

Somewhere between a few days and a few weeks, you become more annoyed by the way things are done in your new locale. During this *Irritability Phase*, you find your frustration tolerance dropping lower and lower. You are now exhibiting various symptoms of "culture shock," which can lead to sleep and appetite disruption, weight loss or gain, inertia and listlessness, unexplained crying, physical complaints, moodiness, feelings of helplessness and loneliness.

The risks of fatigue and disorientation are greater during this stage, predisposing you to increased anxiety, frustration, mistrust, anger, and in extreme cases, loss of touch with reality. Several cases have even been reported in which otherwise peaceful, well-adjusted individuals became violent and psychotic due to the accumulated stress and exhaustion of travel. On some level, each of us can relate to the likelihood of greater volatility and impulsivity under these circumstances. We overreact to minor setbacks, explode when we don't get our way. Feelings of entitlement lead us to demand things that are unreasonable.

What at first seemed quaint and fascinating now appears stupid and uncivilized. You don't belong in this new environment. You are an outsider. Most of all, daily tasks are a real chore to complete. Ultimately, you may reject the foreign culture at this point, and go home relieved you will soon be in familiar surroundings.

If you stick things out, you reach an *Accommodation Phase,* a kind of truce in which your whining and complaining diminish. You have adjusted on a surface level, can find your way around reasonably well, even if you aren't as happy as you had hoped. It is common to feel homesick and to make comparisons continuously between the way you used to do things and the ways you are forced to do them now.

As you learn to make sense of the language, customs, and behavior of the local people, you enter a *Reflective Phase.* Compared to the previous stage where you had been functioning fairly well, you experience setbacks as a result of your consideration of deeper personal issues that are triggered by your travels. Isolation, even alienation and despair, are not unusual. After all, at this point you are confronting significant issues related to where you belong, what you value, and who you are. Although this not an enjoyable period, it *is* interesting and stimulating. With sufficient persistence, resilience, and patience, the pendulum will swing back toward a place where you accept and appreciate things as they are.

If you have stayed in the foreign culture long enough, and worked yourself all the way through the process, you eventually reach an *Adaption Phase.* You may not be able to pass yourself as a native but on most good days you feel like one. You are now adjusted to your surroundings—the people, culture, and weather—in such a way that you have a created a new home within yourself. You may regress at various times to previous stages, depending on life transitions you go through and traumas you suffer, but basically you are doing fine . . . until you leave.

The final *Reentry Phase* includes all the previous ones rearing their heads again as you return home to a culture that will now seem foreign as well as unfamiliar. At first, you will gorge on favorite foods, indulge in things you missed, reconnect with family and friends, feel thankful for what you have. This honeymoon soon gives way to the other stages, one by one, until such time as you have once again resumed a normal state of functioning.

A Spirit of Equanimity

Maintaining a calm and unflappable spirit is crucial during transformative travels. Once you leave behind the tours and tourists, you enter reality with all its delights and horrors. More than anything else, a sense of humor helps you keep things in perspective.

If anyone had a sense of humor about traveling it was Erma Bombeck, who tells this story of a drive through the highlands of Papua New Guinea.

The guide showed her a spot where a plane had crashed. "The natives saw it fall to the ground," he said, "and when they got there, two were still alive."

"They took them to the hospital?" she asked.

"They ate them," he said.

"It gave new meaning to the catch-of-the day," she adds ruefully.

As she lay in bed with her husband, listening to screams and gunshots outside and mosquitoes buzzing inside, Bombeck asked her husband again why they were there. Why, to get away from their normal lives, he explained for the fourth time. They were there to fortify themselves to face another fifty weeks of car repairs and mortgage payments.

———

There are times during travels when, inevitably, you will question why you are not at home rather than stuck in some godforsaken place upstream without a paddle. It is a sense of humor, writes Mary Morris in a book for women on traveling alone, that helps you keep your sanity: "Humor is the traveler's first line of defense. Travel without humor is like sex without love. You can do it, but what's the point, really?"

10

Long-Term Versus Brief Travel

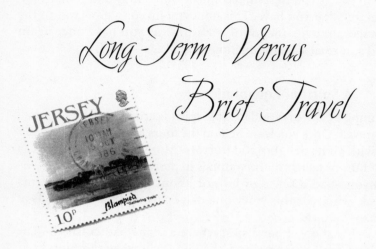

Therapists have debated for years whether real change takes place in a matter of years or weeks. On one side, it's argued that fundamental alterations in a person's character require years of tutoring and hard work. Since the job involves major reconstruction, it is necessary to create a complete blueprint, lay a solid foundation, excavate the past and integrate it into the future, and build slowly and methodically until the job is done properly. Those who hold this view maintain that, as with insight-oriented long-term therapy, producing substantial and lasting changes by means of transformative travel would involve a trip that spanned many months.

On the other side, a different group of change agents claim that if you handle things properly, focus more on action than insight, and work toward specific rather than global goals, you can make a significant difference in your life in a relatively short time. This sort of "brief therapy" is usually measured in a matter of a dozen sessions rather than the traditional year or two.

Since time is at a premium for most people, it is by far the greatest preference to initiate changes in a matter of weeks rather than years. Likewise, as much as people might like to take off for several months to get their act together, they must often make do with a week or two. Obviously, having more time to work on yourself is better than less time. How much time you need depends on several factors, including your personal goals, your financial resources, the nature of your concerns, where you go and how you travel, how hard you work with the time you do have available.

GO LONG

Initially, I will argue that the more time you take for yourself the better the chances that you can not only make some significant changes in your life but also sustain the momentum after you return. After offering some convincing reasons why longer trips are far superior to shorter ones, we will then look more realistically at what you can do within the time parameters that are available to you.

Taking a Sabbatical

The King family of Calgary, Alberta, has been planning for years to take some extended time off to see the world. Mary and Jim decided to take their two daughters out of school for a year and to travel slowly all the way around the planet. They saved their money carefully for four years, banking enough to meet their anticipated expenses. They have constructed a budget, arranged for their home to be cared for and their bills to be paid. They perused maps and read hundreds of guidebooks. They have anticipated every problem they could possibly imagine from stocking a medicine bag to planning the girls' school curriculum.

Despite all the thought and work they've put in, however, each of the King family finds it hard to say just why they are sacrificing so much to make this lengthy trip. Finally, Jim, the dad, explains: "As our departure date approaches, we find ourselves asking, 'What do we hope to gain from this trip; why are we going?' We can't find a firm response that sticks. Perhaps most attractive to us is the possibility of gaining a far more comprehensive feeling for life on this planet."

There are just some goals that can't be reached over a long weekend. You will need time to complete a real transformative adventure— a few months or longer, argues David Sharp, who advocates planning for sabbaticals. There are a lot of excuses why this isn't possible, you could argue. There are family responsibilities and financial obligations. Then there is your job.

Yet taking extended time off isn't as difficult as you might imagine. Some companies—including Xerox, Dupont, and American Express—have even begun programs that allow employees to take as much as a year to pursue outside interests before they return. Although most employers are not nearly as understanding and flexible, most people would have to admit—if they were really honest with themselves—that it isn't a matter of not being able to afford an extended trip, but rather that they choose not to go because they don't want to pay the price.

These same people may think nothing of paying exorbitant mortgage payments or going into debt far beyond what they can comfortably afford just so they can enjoy various luxuries. They will pay out of pocket as much as $5,000 per year for therapy sessions, or $10,000 per year for car payments and expenses, because it makes them feel good. Money, after all, is really about how you choose to spend your time and resources.

Keep in mind, as well, that taking time off by itself is not necessarily transformative; it all depends on what you do with the freedom. In Sharp's words, taking a sabbatical from work is more about looking for a change of perspective rather than of scenery. In his interviews with people who have found a way to travel for extended periods, he spoke with a couple in their thirties who saved their money and spent a year bicycling across South America and a social worker who took a six-month unpaid leave to walk the Pacific Crest Trail from Mexico to Canada. In these cases, and many others, people discovered to their surprise how easy it was to put the plans together. Once you confront your excuses, you find that employers are far more flexible than you imagined. Furthermore, adopting the "road mentality" of sabbatical life means you can actually live cheaper than you can at home. The overall ethic of such travel involves doing without as much as you can, living as simply as you can. You are exchanging a nice car and other extravagances for the freedom to go where you like and do what you want.

Whether island hopping in the South Pacific, becoming a ski bum in the Rockies, bicycling across Europe, or walking the Appalachian Trail, travel sabbaticals change the ways you look at things because they break up your usual routines. Places like the Appalachian Trail are known as a sort of Lourdes for the emotionally overwrought or deprived. Just as some people make pilgrimages to soak their crippled bodies in healing waters, so do others gravitate to places that are supposed to provide spiritual and psychological boosts after a period of time.

Writing about the attractions of walking the Appalachian Trail from Georgia to Maine, Brad Wetzler describes it as "something of a magnet for people whose lives, for one reason or another, are a little out of sync, victims of automobile accidents, bad relationships, corporate downsizing."

He describes some of the characters he met along the way of this three-month journey—Screaming Coyote, a twenty-two-year-old stroke victim who was told he'd never walk again; Houndog, who flunked out of a military academy and was showing his father he was still made of the right stuff; Beorn, weighing in at a hefty 350 pounds, who was trying unsuccessfully to lose weight and stop swearing. All of them declared that when they returned home a few months hence, they would never be the same again. Where they happened to be wasn't what made the difference; it was the commitment to take off a significant amount of time to clear their heads.

Imagining such a sabbatical fantasy is quite common. In one study it was found that 70 percent of people think about taking several months off to travel. Furthermore, among those between the ages of thirty-five and forty-nine, one in five think about it every day!

In *Six Months Off*, Hope Dlugozima and her colleagues describe a number of practical strategies that can be undertaken to make this fantasy a reality. They begin by providing a list of typical reasons people claim such a sabbatical would be out of the question.

- You can't afford it.
- Your employer would never permit it.
- Your family would vehemently oppose the idea.
- You can't just walk away from your responsibilities.
- You have debts to pay off and payments to make.
- It would set your career back.
- You don't have the time.

The authors argue that these are mere excuses that could be overcome if you were sufficiently motivated and creative. The real question is: How committed are you to changing yourself?

As for the very real concerns about finances, time constraints, family and social responsibilities, and career impact, Dlugozima and her colleagues offer a number of options that rest on the assumption that you can take the time to travel if you really want to. Much depends on realigning your priorities, keeping expenses down, compromising with family and coworkers, and confronting your own fears.

Kay Burke uncovered quite a number of individuals who had made their dream a reality. She found a doctor who gave up his practice to sail around the world, a construction worker who built himself a log cabin in the woods, a computer saleswoman who found romance in Kathmandu, a recent widow who bid farewell to her grandchildren and went kayaking around the Hawaiian islands.

Based on her interviews with people who have made successful escapes possible, Burke warns the prospective long-term traveler to plan long in advance in much the same way the King family saved their money. Fantasy begins to take shape as reality, once you get obsessed. This means reading everything you can get your hands on, talking to anyone who will listen, letting yourself believe that you really can take all the time you need. In the words of Wayne Carpenter, a financial writer who hungered for adventure: "You can't believe how easy it is. You just sell your house and go. It seems complicated, even frightening, but in fact it's really very easy."

Of course, some day you will want to return home, and it is that day that you want to prepare for by living as frugally as you can, saving as much as possible, and keeping your future options open.

Overcoming Self-Made Obstacles

It is absolutely terrifying when you consider that time is really all you have in this life; everything else is an illusion. With each heartbeat, another second of your life is gone forever. Every moment you are moving irrevocably closer to your death. Your heart and body are slowly wearing out, even now as you read these words. Feel your heart beating in your chest, a mortal muscle, after all—with each squeeze it is taking another small segment out of the time you have left.

Now ask yourself, given how precious little time you have on this planet, what do you want to do with the heartbeats you still have? Is it really a matter of not having the time to do what you want, or not choosing to spend it to do what you really want? Why do we need to be told we are dying of cancer, with only months left to live, before we choose to take off and see the world? The truth is that each of us *is* operating under a death sentence.

It is also interesting that even when people can take the time off, they tend to be unwilling to disengage themselves from their life routines. This, of course, is the reason they're feeling stuck in the first place, and why they hunger for some sort of transformation.

If there is one enviable thing about life as a university professor, it is that once every seven years you are entitled to one semester off, or even a whole year. Yet even with this subsidized opportunity for travel, most faculty elect not to exercise their options. Isn't that unbelievable! They can have the time off but they don't want it!

I asked several faculty members who had been working at their universities for twenty years or more without a break why they had never taken off the time to which they were entitled. Each of them shrugged and smiled apologetically before offering a feeble excuse that even they didn't believe: "I don't know. It's just too much trouble to arrange things. Besides, I've just got too much to do around here."

Ah, the illusion of indispensability—nobody could do what you do quite as well. This is only one of a number of excuses that works so well in preventing you from taking off the time you need to take care of yourself. Another common reason offered is: "Well, I would like to take some time off, but what would I do? I don't know where to go or how to arrange it."

If that is what's holding you back, here are just a few of the possibilities that have worked out well for people who were looking to change their lives through an extended trip:

- Exchange houses and cars with someone in Europe for the summer.
- Exchange jobs, houses, and cars for a year in Australia with someone in your line of work.
- Work with war refugees in Africa.
- Study intensive Spanish in a Mexican language institute.
- Join the Peace Corps.
- Bicycle across New Zealand.
- Earn your keep as an apprentice at a retreat center in California.
- Work as a volunteer for the National Park Service.
- Build houses for Habitat for Humanity.

- Do research and field studies in an area of interest.
- Work as an au pair.
- Walk the Pacific Crest Trail.
- Work on a kibbutz in Israel.

"Sure," I can hear you saying as you read through this list. "So, I'm supposed to tell my spouse and my children that we're heading off to Botswana?" Or: "I'm just supposed to quit my job and take off for the Great Unknown?" Or: "At my age, I should join the Peace Corps?" Or: "Come on! I could never do these things! I'm not sure I even want to."

I will grant you that a long trip isn't right for everyone. It may not even be necessary, or even desirable, for you to disengage from your normal life to make needed personal changes. As often as not, people take off for extended periods of time not because they are courageous but cowardly. They are running away from intimacy and responsibility. They are escaping from the hard work that is involved in building a solid, rich life and maintaining loving relationships.

The good news is that it isn't necessary to take a sabbatical to transform yourself, nor is it required that you invest a lot of time in the endeavor. The most important thing is how you use the time that you do have available.

Ordinary Moments

We've already heard the stories in which people made fundamental changes in their lives as a result of an adventure that lasted a single afternoon. Likewise, there are people who travel continuously for years who are not any different than before they began the trip.

As we've seen previously, it isn't necessary to go somewhere exotic for a period of months to reap the benefits of transformative travel. Actually, even in remote and spectacular locales, it is often the most ordinary moments that have the greatest impact. On an island off the coast of Hong Kong stands the largest Buddha in the world, bigger than an apartment building. Impressive indeed, I think, but nowhere near as memorable as the sight of two preschool children, sisters, who are sharing one another's ice cream cones.

A tour guide proudly recites all the facts associated with the building of the Hoover Dam, surely one of the great engineering feats of all time. My attention, however, is drawn to the utter stillness of the air.

It doesn't seem to move but just covers everything like an electric blanket turned on high.

Once I went to Portland on a business trip, a routine two-day jaunt for a meeting, and a boring one at that. Before I left, I arranged a ride to the airport from a friend, someone I had known for years. As in so many male friendships, we were close but never spoke of this intimacy directly. Although we frequently met for lunch, or went out together with our wives, we never once talked about our feelings for one another, the closeness we both felt. As he dropped me at the gate, we both turned to one another out of habit, used to hugging our spouses good-bye under such circumstances. Yet in that moment as we each smiled shyly, we acknowledged the deep love we felt—in a way that male friends rarely do.

It didn't matter where I was going, or for how long I was staying, just that I was going somewhere. That act of leaving was the excuse to say good-bye, and in so doing, to express what it means to miss a friend.

It is ordinary moments such as these that make up the most powerful travel experiences. Certainly the more time you take for yourself on a trip, the more opportunities you can create to increase the probability that one of them will knock you for a loop. The first step in doing so is to confront your excuses for not taking the time you really need.

GO SHORT

Okay, you aren't prepared to sell your house and abandon your job, family, friends, and civic responsibilities. But you still want to enjoy the benefits of a trip in a more realistic period of time. You're not alone! Worry not: you would be amazed what you can do in a long weekend.

Even though some lucky people are earning more vacation time with shorter work weeks, people want to do more in a briefer period of time. Modern transportation allows us to move faster, visit more places, see more, do more, and still be home before we're missed. The mentality seems to be that if you can visit more places in the shortest possible period of time, then you have gotten the most value for your money.

As an extreme example of this, I saw one Japanese tour group land in Auckland, New Zealand, in the morning. They took a brief tour of the city, then flew on to Rotorua to see a Maori cultural show and view the volcanic activity in the bubbling pools. Then they flew on to the South Island where they had lunch on Mount Cook. Small planes dropped them off on the Tasman Glacier where they walked around a bit, then flew back to the local airport where they boarded another flight to see the fjords off Milford Sound. They landed in Queenstown for dinner, where the local stores catering to Japanese tourists stayed open late so they could fill their bags with souvenirs before they headed onward to Australia the next morning. They saw the whole country in a single day!

Don't laugh too hard. We all do the same thing in our own way—try to pack in as much as we can into the limited time available. In fact, we may even judge the success of a trip by how many different things we did in the shortest period of time.

It is perhaps ironic that continuous, frantic action does not necessarily transform us; in many ways, it even *prevents* change because there is so little time for reflection, so few opportunities to digest experiences and integrate them—everything runs together. Transformative travel can be short in duration, but it takes a different approach from the marathon collection of sights and souvenirs.

Brief Travel

One of the problems of modern life is that there is never enough time to do everything that you would like. Because you are harried and rushed, you need vacation breaks more than ever. Unfortunately, for most people the prospect of taking a lengthy trip of a month or more is only a dream; even a week away from home places undue hardship on some.

Fear not, however. We live in the age of *brief* therapy. It is no longer fashionable to spend years in analysis to change yourself; now you can do it in a matter of weeks. Part of the impetus for this change in strategy comes from economic necessity—skyrocketing medical costs and abuses of the system. Managed care organizations are now dictating to people whether their problems warrant treatment, and if so, how long they have to put things in proper order. Whereas once upon a time, *good* therapy took a minimum of six months, and usually a year or more, nowadays some problems may be addressed quite effectively in a fraction of that time.

The other reason why forms of brief therapy are becoming increasingly popular is because that is what consumers demand. People are feeling impatient with slow, steady progress. They want to see some results quickly. I have had more than a few new patients ask me in a first interview how long it will take us to resolve the depression or anxiety that they have been struggling with their whole lives. "Will we be able to take care of this today? Or will I have to come back for another session?"

The same could be said for transformative travel. "Okay, I like the idea of this stuff. I *would* like to change my life in some significant ways. I'd rather not go to a therapist. It's expensive. And embarrassing. Besides, it takes too long. I'm in a hurry. So, if I take a few days off from work next week, how do I get things rolling?"

If the goal is to create transformative travel experiences in a matter of days rather than weeks, it's best to follow the same principles that apply to brief therapy.

• *Define the problem.* Make sure you frame the problem in a way that allows it to be solved in a short period of time. In other words, keep your goals realistic given the amount of time available to work on them. There is a big difference between saying you want less conflict in your life (which is often difficult to control and takes a very long time) and saying you want to change the ways you react to conflicts with a particular person.

As one person describes, sometimes a brief trip can help you define exactly what the problem is that you are struggling with:

> One of my crystallizing moments came on a nice, sunny fall afternoon visiting Zion National Park. I was in a nice relationship, with possibly a marriage in the future. I had been aware that something was off, but could not quite pinpoint what it was. In the tranquil surroundings the understanding came to me: she disturbed my peace. I can still visualize walking up a trail, alone, to search for the peace I needed. I was alone, serenity all around me. The surroundings gave me my peace back and I decided that her power to upset me stops here. I saw clearly what my life would be five or ten years from now if I didn't change direction. My love was secondary to my need for inner peace.

• *Define your goals.* Once the objective is identified, the next step is to establish goals. Brief efforts are more likely to be successful when your objectives are limited, specific, and realistic. Focus on one facet of your life you would like to work on, concentrating on that dimension above all others.

What are some areas that people most frequently target? They want time away from major relationships to put them into perspective and make decisions for the future. They want to lose weight and start a regular exercise program. They want to meet someone special. They want to work on forgiveness in those relationships in which they feel they have been hurt. They want some decompression time to heal. Or perhaps they just want to initiate some changes in lifestyle.

Valerie combined a few extra days of vacation with a brief business trip to Salt Lake City, a place she had never visited before. It is not so much that she wanted a break from work as she needed some time away from her usual routines to make some sort of decision about where she was headed in her life. She jotted down on a napkin during one boring meeting some specific areas in which she felt most uncertain. It seemed reasonable to her that decisive action could be taken in each of them, if she only knew what she wanted to do.

The next thing she did was purchase a brand new pair of hiking boots, a task she found surprisingly satisfying in its own right. She loved the look and feel of them. Most of all, she appreciated what they represented: freedom to walk her own way.

Outfitted in her new boots, carrying a picnic lunch and water bottle, she followed a well-marked trail out of Park City until she found a secluded spot. There she spent the whole day watching a waterfall, feeding birds some of her nuts and raisins, mostly just sorting out what she wanted to do. She was determined not to come down off the mountain until she had made some firm decisions.

It wasn't until it began to get cold, with the sky darkening, that she finally took a stand in all three areas, writing down her commitments on the same napkin that helped launch her journey. As she started back down toward civilization, with her feet sore from breaking in a new pair of boots, she smiled at the surprise she would bring to her family and friends once they heard about her day and what it had spawned.

• *Ask yourself what would be different if you transformed yourself?* In the parlance of the solution-focused therapy invented by William O'Hanlon and others, this is called the "miracle question." It encourages you to imagine a time in the future when you have arrived at where you want to be. If you woke up tomorrow and your problem was solved, what would you notice first? How would others respond to you? How exactly did you manage to make these changes happen?

This strategy is a tricky one, for it forces you to say aloud what you need to do, even though you may feel reluctant to commit yourself. The simple act of imagining a solution acts as a catalyst to make it happen.

It is common, for example, that when you ask someone what they need to do, they will typically say: "Gee, I don't know." Rather than letting it go at that, try prompting further with encouragement to take a wild guess. You will be amazed at how often once people are let off the hook, given permission to guess without knowing positively and absolutely, they will supply the exact solution they need to follow to resolve things satisfactorily. In other words, people often do know what is best for themselves, and what they need to do to make their lives better, even if they struggle to put these hunches into words.

Ellis feels confused and uncertain about what he wants to do in his relationship with his daughter. She wants to drop out of school for a while, an action he believes is ludicrous. When he tries to talk with her about the decision, it invariably ends in an argument. He isn't sure whether to cut off all financial assistance or continue to support her during this transition. He doesn't know whether to give her space or push her harder. He agonizes about his options, back and forth continuously, unsure about what to do and how to do it.

When he imagines a time in which they have resolved their conflict (a task he is most resistant to complete), Ellis pictures a time five years in the future. They treat one another with respect. They. . . . His fantasy is interrupted with the follow-up question: "So, how did you work things out?"

Whatever answers Ellis supplies provide the clues as to what he needs to do next. In this case, it was taking his daughter away for a few days, just the two of them, that broke through the impasse. They got in the car without even looking at a map and just headed toward the horizon. They got to know one another better, studiously avoided the issue at hand. Yet the more time they spent together driving along the highway, giggling and telling stories, the less of a wedge this particular conflict made in their relationship.

• *Stay in the present.* Leave the past behind. It is the luxury of time that allows you to dip into the past, to dwell on your life themes, to analyze and make sense of what you have lived before. That is why traditional therapy often takes such a long time: It is a major undertaking to review everything that has led you to this point in your life, to uncover aspects of your experience you have forgotten or neglected, and then to integrate all of this into a coherent view of yourself and where you are headed.

In brief therapeutic travel, like brief therapy, there is little time to consider the past. Furthermore, according to this particular method, the past gets in the way of the present. Who cares how or why you ended up in this particular situation at this moment? The point is what you're going to do to get yourself out of it.

Of course there is some merit to looking back, especially if you want to figure out your mistakes so you don't repeat them, or if you are motivated by a quest for self-understanding. This mission, however, will have to be undertaken during another time when you are not feeling so impatient. For now, your task is to figure out what you can change today, in this moment.

Cody has spent a lifetime in therapy, ever since high school when he first began struggling with his parents' divorce and his low academic achievement and self-esteem. In fact, he quite likes therapy. Over the course of treatment with three or four different practitioners, Cody has learned a lot about himself. He enjoys the frank and stimulating discussions with bright, sensitive, and perceptive professionals. He appreciates the weekly structure in his life in which he feels accountable to someone for his actions. Most of all, he enjoys the challenge of trying to make sense of his life.

Cody can articulate quite clearly the reasons that his father's early abuse, his mother's alcoholism, and their subsequent divorce undermined his sense of competence. With little prompting, he can tell you about a number of unconscious desires that he has uncovered, several characteristic defenses that are counterproductive, and the major struggle of his life to find true intimacy with another. The problem, though, is that he hasn't had a date in months and a long-term relationship in years.

Although he intended to continue with his therapy and his excavations into the past, he decided to take a vacation from both the sessions and his normal life. He booked a trip to a resort frequented by single people of his age and interests. Furthermore, he decided during the plane ride that he would leave the old Cody behind during this adventure. He would not think about the past but only the present. Each time he was presented with an opportunity to approach an attractive woman, he would not analyze things, he would not mull over his past failures, nor would he think endlessly about what options he had and what they might mean; he would simply act.

Not surprisingly, Cody was able to break old patterns by creating new options for himself. As long as he was in this enriched environment away from home and the influences that usually stifled him, he was able to build a number of new relationships. Of course, one problem with staying only in the present for a short period of time is that he didn't manage to maintain any of these relationships beyond a brief interlude. Even more challenging would be to continue these new patterns once he returns home, hopefully a strategy that his therapist will be able to help him with.

• *Look for exceptions*. When mired in difficult situations, people typically dwell on what is going wrong rather than what is going right. Even therapists fall into this trap by encouraging their patients to talk always about their problems and what they are struggling with instead of balancing these failures with an equal number of successes. When the ledger is added up, it usually feels like things are worse than they really are.

Dana says she is depressed. That label makes it sound as if the word defines her, as if she *is* depression. In addition, *being* depressed is far different from *acting* depressed under some circumstances. In fact, very few of us are depressed all the time, and even if that was true, there are degrees of depression in which you feel better at some times rather than others.

All her life, Dana has taught people around her to expect that most of the time she is in a pretty low mood. The key word in this description is *most*, since it implies there are indeed times when she is not depressed even if they are relatively rare. On an unconscious level, Dana even enjoys her predicament because people expect so little of her. Whenever she doesn't feel like doing something or doesn't want to exert herself, she just tells people she isn't feeling well and they seem to understand even if they occasionally grumble a bit.

During a brief trip to visit a relative, someone who didn't know that Dana was supposed to be depressed all the time, she noticed that one afternoon she was positively glowing with excitement. This was indeed an exception for her, but a situation the people with whom she was with thought was normal. They just assumed that Dana was always so carefree.

What Dana proved to herself on this adventure is that she was capable of being "not depressed" in the right situation. Once she began looking at her behavior more carefully, focusing on the times when she was doing well rather than poorly, she found a number of other exceptions.

Since during travels you are away from the usual cues, situations, and contexts that elicit the behavior you would like to change, you are more likely to find exceptions in which you act in fully functioning ways. This is especially true if you adopt a mindset in which you look for such instances.

Like most brief therapy strategies, the solution is a simple one: Figure out what you are doing that has worked before and then do it again.

• *Take small steps.* Little changes lead to big changes. Often it feels overwhelming to think about changing patterns that have become entrenched over a lifetime. If, however, you can make even a tiny alteration in your behavior, in *any* direction, you prove that things are potentially within your control. If you can change the rate of your behavior, its duration or intensity, its sequence or location, you set in motion the possibility of making more substantial changes later.

So often during change efforts, you get to the point where you feel stuck and discouraged. Given that you are working under limited time parameters, you want to make sure that the therapeutic goals you pursue are attainable. If, for example, you wanted to lose weight during a trip, and keep it off after you return, you could work on changing one small part of your eating cycle. This could include eating with your left hand, or with the plate six inches further away from you, or at different times of the day. It doesn't matter so much what you do as long as you change a little something about the way you do things. If the strategy works, keep doing it; if it doesn't, try something else.

• *Do the opposite.* When you are stuck doing something that isn't working, you tend to repeat those ineffectual actions. Getting back to weight loss, if you kept trying to shed pounds by going on radical diets, you might discover that, whereas your initial efforts were successful, the lost pounds eventually piled back on. After trying that strategy unsuccessfully several times, it would seem apparent that diets don't really work well over the long haul.

The opposite of going on a diet is *not* going on a diet, meaning that you avoid making any changes in your eating habits that you are not prepared to maintain for the rest of your life. Will this work? Perhaps not. The intent, however, is to avoid repeating strategies that you know have not worked before so that you are free to experiment with other alternatives that, in the right combination, will prove helpful.

The major premise of brief therapy is that it is important to remain flexible. Since travel constantly puts you into situations in which you have to experiment just to get through the day, it is the perfect setting in which to try new behaviors that are often the opposite of what you would normally do.

• *Shake things up.* Since time is at a premium, you don't have the luxury of messing around. During lengthier trips you can dally about, dip your toe in the water, see how it feels, think about if you want to submerge yourself deeper, work up the courage, take a deep breath, dip in your whole foot, and so on. When you only have a few minutes, though, and you really want to swim, you just jump in. This strategy may be shocking and unpleasant for a little while, but hey, *you* are the one who wants to change quickly.

On briefer trips, you have to build into each day, if not each hour, some therapeutic tasks that are going to shake you up and get you going in the right direction. This is a kind of "shock treatment" that you attempt when baby steps are not working or not appropriate. This also accounts for how brief therapy can often initiate changes just as sweeping as lengthier traditional therapies. People are required to complete tasks between sessions that stir things up and help them practice new skills they are learning. During brief transformative travel, as well, it is absolutely critical that you not only think about your life and talk about things you want to do, but also that you act in new ways.

To continue the swimming metaphor, if you are after fast, significant changes in your life, then you can't expect satisfactory results by dipping your toe into the cultures you visit; you have to jump in with both feet.

With only a few weeks, or even days, to stir things up and construct new patterns, there is little time to sit around musing about things. In the kind of travel that produces significant changes, you must balance a certain amount of contemplation with decisive action. Yet action, by itself, without considerable reflection on the meaning of your experience, is also unlikely to produce lasting changes that alter your existence to its deepest core.

11

Creating Meaning in Your Travel

*Y*our journey is only half over once you return home. The first part of any trip involves the actual physical travel; equally important is what you recollect about the experience and what meaning you assign to it.

Meaning for any given person is not so much related to a travel event's physical reality, or even its authenticity, but rather to how it is perceived. Someone can look at the Las Vegas strip as the ultimate in human degradation and plasticity, or as a campy postmodern festival of creativity. Similarly, walking among the Grand Tetons can provide spiritual transcendence for one person and a collection of blisters for another. The key to any travel experience is thus related to whatever meaning you give it.

THE PERCEPTION OF EXPERIENCE

It is difficult to tell, objectively, whether a particular event will be significant for you or not until we know your state of mind and the context for the experience. It is perplexing and fascinating how two people can each face the same circumstances with such different responses to what they experienced. A husband and wife, for example, both walk together to the top of a cliff overlooking the sea. The man finds the view merely pretty, perhaps even exhilarating, but the woman feels transformed: "I could feel, at that moment, how truly insignificant I am. The things I worry about really don't matter much in the grand scheme of things. The ocean doesn't care what I do. When we walked back to town, it felt like everything was different."

While many factors affect the extent to which a particular travel incident will influence you, much depends on the focus of your awareness—of what is going on around you as well as within you. A number of questions come immediately to mind as relevant: What do you notice most vividly about the scene? What strikes you as worthy of closer scrutiny? How does this event connect with others that come to mind? What is getting in the way of you doing more with what you have seen and felt?

Expectations, Assumptions, and Beliefs

There are indeed barriers that interfere with your ability to get the most out of any experience. You hold certain beliefs about what is possible, many of which are self-limiting. Your emotional state and receptivity at any moment also make you more or less willing to expand your horizons. At times you feel quite open whereas at others you are distracted. There is also a context for your experience; you can't look at anything in isolation, any single event disconnected from what proceeded it.

Transformative travel is a cumulative phenomenon. It is a culmination of prior learning. It builds on a succession of experiences that have, independently and collectively, nudged you to the exact point where you are open to a dramatic surge forward.

You are walking the streets of a strange city. Quite by accident, you find yourself in animated conversation with a homeless person, someone who is not interested in handouts but rather in intelligent dialogue about a recent news event. You walk away from the encounter profoundly moved by what you just experienced, on many different levels.

First of all, you changed your opinion on a pure cognitive level about the subject you had been discussing. This woman had an impact on you in other ways as well, many of which you can barely grasp. You feel a new commitment to reach out to others in the future. You are now more willing to look beyond surface appearances in forming impressions of others. Perhaps most significant of all: you now intend to make some changes in your life as a result of this serendipitous encounter. You are determined to simplify your life when you return home. There was something about the free spirit of the woman that spoke to you convincingly.

It would seem, on first glance, that this single travel event—speaking to a woman on the street—produced transformative growth. Indeed, this interaction was a powerful catalyst. But here was a history and context that played a major role in this change. Hundreds of other conversations led up to this moment.

Why now? Why at that moment, in that particular place, did this woman produce so profound an effect on you?

The answers are found in the particular meaning ascribed to the experience. If someone else encountered the same street person, it is doubtful that he or she would have been altered in the same way. That person might have labeled the encounter as distasteful rather than enlightening.

Depending on the expectations, assumptions, and beliefs you bring to any critical moment, you will be predisposed to change in ways that others would not. For evidence of this proposition, you would only have to look at the multitude of ways that a group of people react to the same situations.

A tour group of thirty travelers is informed their charter flight has been delayed several hours. They all have to be at the same place at the same time, so there is no reason to believe this setback is more disappointing to one person than to another. Yet their reactions to the delay are diverse. A few people go ballistic; they rant and rave, threaten and cajole, as if somehow that will get things going faster. A few others mutter silently to themselves, anxiety written on their faces. Another contingent shrugs unconcernedly, burying themselves in books or magazines to wait out the delay. One final group reacts as strangely as the first, but in the opposite direction. Rather than acting aggravated or disappointed by the delay, they whoop with joy. A few head for the bar determined to start this holiday wherever they happen to be. A few others, even more adventurous, hire a taxi to spend a few hours looking around.

Each of these distinctly different reactions is shaped by unique interpretations of what took place. We can, therefore, conclude that regardless of your personal mood and circumstances, much depends on what meaning you give to any experience, whether it is a delayed flight or an encounter with a person on the street.

Constructing Experience

One of the most influential movements in education and the social sciences is *constructivism,* a theory that examines all human behavior in its larger social and cultural contexts. It is presumed that there really is no objective reality to speak of, at least as far as human perception is concerned. Everything you know, believe, understand, and experience is shaped by influences from your family, ethnicity, religion, cultural heritage, politics, language, education, and exposure to the media.

In a sense, personal change, whether during travel or in any other setting, occurs because the person acknowledges and labels the experience in a particular way. Depending on your preexisting mindset and the filters with which you view what is happening, any series of events can be seen as inconsequential or significant. In one sense, what this book is intended to do is to help you construct meaning in experiences that otherwise might pass you by. In other words, it may not be necessary for you to change the way you travel as much as to alter and enhance the ways you reflect on your journeys.

The act of rock climbing, for example, isn't over until the events are relived and the tale is told. In his book on the psychology of adventure, Richard Mitchell explains: "The meaning of mountaineering events emerges in the reflective discussion and debate that follow them." These debriefings serve several purposes. Unique to this particular competitive activity, fellow climbers rate the relative merits of the ascent, that is, they judge collectively its degree of worthiness. Second, climbers review their route, discussing not only where they went but where they could have gone. This is about coulds, shoulds, and might-have-beens, but it is also a way to learn and improve skills and performance in the future—and it is the way status is assigned. Third, debriefings create a climate of cohesion and camaraderie that is at least as pleasurable as the climb itself. Support is offered as needed, and teasing as well, in a spirit of good humor.

Mitchell ends his study of mountaineering motives with this conclusion:

> While looking for happiness and fulfillment, some of us find mountains. If, in climbing them, we feel and become more than was possible

before, let us not forget whom to praise. It is not the stones that make us happy. They provide no memories or sense of completion. Whatever we find in the mountains we took there in the first place. In the end the mountains do not care what experiences we make of them. They are nothing but wrinkles on a shifting crust, frozen water upon water, dust upon dust—nothing—until men and women come to give them meaning.

What You Remember

As we've seen in the example of mountaineering, travels are not just lived once but again and again as you retell the stories of your adventures. You have flashbacks of particular images that are indelibly burned into your brain. You have photographs you can review at your leisure that freeze representative moments of the experience. As your eye catches a special souvenir or artifact you collected, you're flooded once again by intense associations with that object. Most of all, you have the stories to tell.

If the object of transformative travel is not only to change you significantly but to make those changes endure over time, then their relative power is directly related to how much you remember about the experiences. So many trips you've had in your life have faded, so many resolutions you have made are long forgotten. To make travel transformative, it isn't just what you do, but how you reflect on the experience, what you tell yourself and others about what things mean.

Sometimes there is a significantly delayed effect that can last through months or even years of intensive thought about what happened and how it's connected to your life. One person, for example, had been visiting Rio de Janeiro when the first seeds of change were planted, although it took years for her to make sense of what she had witnessed.

From my plush hotel room in Rio I was able to look through binoculars and see the devastation of a half million people living in shacks. The contrast was startling compared to where I was staying, where I'd been eating, and the spectacular scenery I had been visiting.

At the time, and for several weeks later, I told myself and others who heard my story that the situation was pretty awful but it ended there. Or at least I thought it did.

Over the next several months, I continued to be haunted by the images of the dilapidated slums. I began thinking more and more about how some people have so little while others have so much. I don't know why someone is born poor, lives in a shack, and eats nothing but beans. Yet I have so much.

My values about what is important changed dramatically as a result of that trip, although it took years for me to sort it all out. I understand now that we are all connected. Caring matters. How we relate to others matters. I realize how important it is for me to give of myself. Things and possessions don't matter much anymore. I can make a great difference in the world through my acts of giving and now I know that.

Learning from Others' Stories

Direct experience is only one part of travel; the other is hearing the stories of people we meet along the way. As a race, we human beings are fascinated by stories. Our brains have evolved in such a way that we think in terms of narratives. We invented language and writing as ways to record the best stories we ever heard, those we want to pass along to others. Among the Aboriginals of Australia, and many other indigenous peoples who never employed written records, it is through songs, dances, and oral tales that wisdom is passed on from one generation to the next. Such stories are entertaining, most certainly, but they are also the legacy of the past, chock full of lessons that help people learn from prior experience.

Surely one of the most fascinating aspects of travel is hearing the local stories of the area, as well as the particular legends of any family. Travel adventures arise not just from river rafting and rock climbing but from the stories you hear of those you meet. People around the world want to tell you these tales, if you are open and available to hear them.

Since a skilled story teller is a rare artist, it's your challenge to find those individuals who are curators of the most colorful and informative narratives. These are people who not only know good stories but can tell them in a way that is reasonably accurate, is sufficiently compelling so the tale's significance is evident, and is specifically designed for *you*. And as the interviewer, you must get people to open themselves up in a way that they are willing to reveal their best stuff.

Therapists do this for a living. We are very efficient in getting people to tell us what they have never told anyone before, and to do so in
a short period of time. We do this by getting people to trust us, but
mostly by communicating our sincere interest in hearing what they
have to say. "Help me understand your world," is a polite, respectful,
yet persistent message. People want to tell us their secrets because we
are good listeners, because we don't judge what we hear (at least
overtly), and most of all, because we are safe. But remember: besides a
therapist there is nobody safer than a stranger from out of town.

If you are interested and open, reasonably skilled as a listener and
prompter, you can easily gain access to the best stories of any place
you visit. Keep in mind, however, that one way you build openness in
a relationship is by revealing yourself as well. That is even better for
you, if change is what you are after. If it's safe for strangers to tell you
their secrets, then it's safe for you to tell them yours. Freud discovered
long ago that people feel much better when they are able to tell someone else about their innermost feelings and fantasies. That's one reason people pay for a therapist's time—they are renting an hour of
safety in which they can say aloud what they feel and fear most
intensely, without concern for being judged or written off in the
process. Similarly, you can take risks with people you will never see
again that you wouldn't dream of taking with those you must face day
after day.

FINDING MEANING THROUGH A JOURNAL

Travel journals have taken many forms throughout the ages. In the earliest development, cave walls were used to record highlights of journeys—animals observed, acts of heroism portrayed, strange phenomena
noted. Since then, there has been a long and honored tradition of travel
memoirs—of naturalists (Charles Darwin), sailors (Christopher
Columbus), scientists (Sigmund Freud), or anthropologists (Margaret
Mead). Whereas sometimes we can find evidence of personal transformation in the writings of historical personages (Lawrence of Arabia,
James Cook), it was not their stated objective to travel for the sake of
personal enlightenment.

Eric Leed notes that it was the era of scientific travel in the eighteenth century, characterized by the writings of physicians, scientists,
and sailors, that brought reports of journeys into prominence. Standard methodologies were developed in which the traveler would

record sequences of events in precise detail or systematic collections of all that was known about a place or a people. In the tradition of Darwin's journals, the classic travel journal described, named, and classified everything that was observed.

The very best thing to write about is not where you have been, or where you are going, but rather what you are experiencing at the moment. The superficial details about your travels, or even the events themselves, are far less important to record than your reactions to them.

Your goal is to capture the full essence of your movement through space and time. You are trying to grab hold of the most elusive human experience of all—that of evolution from one state of being to another. For this narrative to be of any use to you, you must be able to get down accurately and completely what is happening not just on the outside but the inside. Travel, perhaps more than any other activity, forces you to attend to and integrate all dimensions of experience into a complex understanding of the world and your place in it.

We know that what produces significant learning experiences for people is not just strategic moments of opportunity but also structures by which to incorporate new insights into ways of being and functioning. Teachers and therapists are constantly figuring out ways to help people articulate what they know, to apply concepts to novel situations, to help them make what they learned part of them. The same holds true if the goal is to convert ordinary travels into significant learning experiences.

Structuring a Journal

Anthropologists keep field notes as a way to record their observations for later reflection and analysis. Human memory is notoriously unreliable. Writing down descriptions of events, perceptions of what transpired, sketches of people and places, impressions of cultural practices, records of internal feelings and thoughts, provides the material that is needed for later recall when you wish to make sense of what you lived through.

Keeping a journal is not only a useful tool for the field scientist but for any of us who wish to be more deliberate and proactive in promoting significant learning experiences from our travels. It is in such a repository that we may record our reactions to what we are observing, resolutions for what we intend to do differently in the future, ideas for intriguing instructional strategies, insights we wish to hang onto, unresolved issues triggered by challenges we face, magical moments we wish to keep for posterity.

Like anthropologists, we capture and process data so we can access it in the future in much the same way we might consult a photo album to rekindle poignant memories. However, unlike photographs, your field notes include your distinct voice expressing significant musings that may otherwise disappear from your consciousness.

I have included a few representative journal entries as samples of the ways that such written reflections can be used to promote personal growth. The first entry, written more than decade ago while I was teaching in Peru, is typical of a particular stance I try to take when I am viewing a new culture. I try to describe, as fully as possible, the scenes around me:

> I spent the past hour talking to Javier, an eleven-year-old boy who seemed knowledgeable about everything—politics, oil, tourism. He also taught me some tricks on his yo yo.
>
> It felt so fine sitting in the park, under the warm sun, passing the day in a language that is almost starting to sound familiar. Now I am sipping on coca tea, reflecting on the barrage of things I have seen today. Funny how the ruins—inanimate creations left by an extinct people—don't leave as powerful an impression as the living people who are here. Farmers. Dirty, shoeless, laughing children kicking around two-thirds of what was once a ball. Women shepherds in their colorful clothes, stout bodies, guiding the llamas down the sides of steep mountainsides. Everyone is selling something—blankets, sweaters, beads. And those with nothing to sell cheerfully and proudly ask for tips to take their pictures.

Essentially neutral in tone, such field notes are like photographs, recording images that you wish to save for future reference. The excitement of the author is certainly evident, his glee over the novel mix of sights and smells. Yet you are reminded that you don't have to be somewhere exotic like Peru to attend more fully to everything that is going on around you.

The next entry, recorded just a few weeks later, was written less about what happened on the outside than about some changes going on in the inside. By now, I had settled into the routines of my teaching job and was making a number of comparisons between what I was used to and what I was then doing.

My first student just stopped by the office during visiting hours (funny, I don't feel like I'm in a hospital). The students seem to be so curious about how things are different in my country. They want to know everything. It is so exciting to introduce them to new ideas and watch their brains ricocheting with excitement. Yet other students seem really threatened by stuff that doesn't fit into what they already thought was true.

I walked with the student to the library, picked out a few books for her on what we had been talking about, and watched her sail away to the nearest sanctuary. I forgot how much fun it is to really teach. I love being here, walking around feeling part of this place. It is as if I have regained my innocence, my virginity, my freshness. I'm trying to remember if I felt this way when I first started out in the field. I don't think so: I was too scared and intimidated to feel anything.

It often seems necessary to transplant yourself into another culture to see clearly the ways you function in your own world. You don't realize how much you need structure in your life until it is gone. You don't know how stale and bored you might feel with the routines of your life until they are disrupted. It is ironic that by immersing yourself in another culture, whether it is across the world or just down the street, you are able to look more clearly inside yourself. In this next field note, I recorded a major self-revelation, one that to this day still reverberates inside my brain:

Insight #1482 in my Peruvian soul-searching: I constantly punish myself, deliver doses of work detail or retribution, when I don't perform as a truly adequate Jeffrey should. It occurred to me as I sit here at my desk laboriously reading a technical article in Spanish, not for its enjoyment or information, but compulsively to keep up my word lists. This is part of my "hard labor" for not speaking up to par in my class today. While the first hour went fabulously as I lectured fluently, interjected humor, acted out pantomimes of images I couldn't describe, I stumbled over a question that I didn't fully understand. For the hour after that my confidence dwindled and my speaking faltered. I'm certain the students noticed next to nothing, but I felt crushed.

Things to Include

Journal entries such as these aid the traveler to internalize the cultural learnings that transpire on a daily basis. There are quite a number of other ways that you can use field notes to help you create meaning from your experiences:

- *Vivid portraits.* These are impressionistic creations that reveal as much about your state of mind and perceptual acuity as they do your subject. Try to describe the essence of things.

- *Representative snapshots.* Just as in a photograph, you are capturing experience—only with words rather than with light. You are exercising not only your descriptive skills but also your focused concentration. What you choose to capture is also revealing about your interests.

- *Connections to the past.* Link what you are experiencing in the present with what you have lived previously. Draw connections between themes that have repeated themselves in your life again and again.

- *Revelations and insights.* This is where you catalogue all the transformative ideas that you have along the way. This includes new things you have realized about yourself.

- *Heightened awareness.* Note anything that you have never noticed before. You will be surprised at a later time how various fragments will come together to form a revelation.

- *Challenges faced.* Write an honest portrayal of the difficulties you encountered and how you handled yourself. Be especially frank about ways you could improve in the future.

- *Internal states of disorder.* This is where you talk about your fears, apprehensions, worries. You use your journal to dump all the ugliest parts of yourself rumbling around inside. Later, when you reread these sections, you will feel especially motivated to excise the aspects thus revealed.

- *Passion.* Talk about that which you feel most passionate. Write about your most creative ideas, your most intense feelings, and your most moving experiences.

- *Dialogue.* Talk with the people you left behind. In the safety of your journal, tell them some about the things you have always wanted to say but held back. Also, talk with yourself about any decisions you are wrestling with, taking both sides of the issues.

- *New skills.* For changes to last, you have to practice new ways of thinking and feeling, new ways of talking to yourself. Use your journal as a dress rehearsal before live performances that have less room for mistakes.

- *Notes to yourself.* More conventionally, you can use the journal to write reminders of things to do when you get back. This allows you to put them out of your mind so you can concentrate more fully on what you are experiencing in the present.

- *Declarations of commitment.* What will you do when you return? What do you resolve to do differently after the trip is over? Accountability to yourself is critical for following through with your intentions.

Writing can play a major role in helping you heighten transformative travel effects. Toby Fulwiler teaches writing as the principal means for promoting any type of active learning. He considers it as "an essential activity to create order from chaos, sense from nonsense, meaning from confusion."

In jotting down your travel impressions, it is important to remember the limits of such internal dialogues. Keep three things in mind:

1. Talking about things isn't a substitute for action.

2. Whining and complaining aren't useful if they get out of control.

3. Solitary reflection shouldn't exclude intimate communication with others.

While it isn't necessary for you to become a professional travel writer to enjoy the benefits of a journalist's heightened perspective on things, the act of describing what you see, sense, and feel does allow you to return to favorite places whenever you want to. Furthermore, just as a photographer looks at the world through a viewpoint in which colors, shadows, textures, and composition are all heightened, so too does seeing the world through a travel writer's lens increase your awareness of details you might otherwise miss.

The challenge of trying to describe the perfect azure blue of the sea against the contrast of blinding white sand, or the chaos of sounds percolating on a busy street, forces you to attend more carefully to everything you observe. The simple act of trying to write or paint what you see intensifies your appreciation for every moment. Even if nobody else ever reads what you write, you have continued access to any scene you care to revisit. This is especially important once you return home, your memories start to fade, and whatever commitments you thought were so useful now seem but a dream.

COMING HOME

It's one thing to transform yourself while you are away from home; the hard part is to make the changes last once you are back on familiar terrain. Under the conditions of maximum serenity that are part of resort life, it is easy to make resolutions you wish to keep. Let's say, for instance, that you decide to build into your life more opportunities for rejuvenation. You work too hard without sufficient time for recovery and reflection. In spite of your best intentions, a week after you return home, you are already back into the same old grind, already cloudy about what it was you thought was so important. Once you reenter the environment you left, as basically the same person you were before, you slip back immediately into the old patterns. Nothing really changes, in part, because people in your life may not want you to change.

Transformative travel experiences are unnerving, not just for you but for others. People expect you to be what you have always been; they don't like it when they have to get used to someone else. After returning from a trip into a stimulating culture, you want to tell everyone about what now feels different. You suspect they won't understand. After all, *you* have been there and they haven't. And you are right—they won't understand the magnitude of what you have been through nor what it all means.

In this final section of the book we look at the challenges involved in returning home, the experience of reentry to your previous life, and how to keep your commitments to follow through on personal changes. In addition, we examine ways that you can promote transformative travel without ever leaving home.

Home Sweet Home

One of the automatic benefits of travel is that if you stay away long enough, you can't wait to come home. Sleep in your own bed. Catch up with family and friends. Find out what happened while you were away. Of course, this comfort and relief lasts only a few days before you begin planning your next trip.

Before future fantasies take root, you do revel in the joys of the familiar. It's true that you often must leave something to appreciate fully how much it means to you. There are so many aspects of your life that you take for granted. A good cup of coffee or milkshake doesn't rate much of your attention—until you can't find one. You might not even drink milkshakes at home, but once you know you can't have one, you start craving them. The same is true with any particular convenience or relationship.

Travel is thus transformative not only in the ways it pushes you to change but in the manner in which it helps you appreciate the joys of *not* changing. After all, it is perspective that you gain when you are away from things most familiar. You realize that you don't miss certain facets of your life—a job, a friendship, a routine—and this leads you to take inventory of what is most important, reorder priorities and make new choices. Just as often, you find out what you miss the most. Absence makes the heart grow fonder *if* you reach the time threshold where longing begins, and if deep down inside you this person or thing is really something that you value.

I love my pillow because I know how poorly I sleep when I don't have it around. On the other hand, I learned—after living out of a small suitcase for three months on the road—how little clothes mean to me. In spite of accumulating a closet full of suits, shoes, and fancy clothes, I now wear variations of only a few basic outfits. I didn't know that I cared little about clothes until I didn't have much around me and it didn't matter.

Likewise, there are a dozen different facets of your life that you think are important. You spend lots of time thinking about these things, plotting to get more of them. Perhaps a few items really are important to you. But one way you can find out for sure is to leave them behind for a while and then note how you feel.

The experience of coming home forces you to confront the things and people most important in your life. That is only one of many reasons why returning from a trip is often stressful as you reenter your old life.

Stresses of Reentry

It has been said by experienced travelers that the most difficult part of any journey is adapting to life back home. One of the reasons for this phenomenon appears to be that people around you are not prepared for the adjustments they will have to make.

For those who have been away for extended periods, there is a feeling of being left behind. You are no longer culturally literate if you haven't been reading local papers, seeing current films and television shows, staying abreast with the latest gossip in the community.

You may be different when you return—but so is everyone else in their own view. Frankly, they aren't all that interested in your stories. Many people will feel jealous, even threatened by what you experienced. They may show polite interest but you can tell they don't really care.

It is also disturbing to see how little has changed since you have been away. People are doing pretty much the same things the same way. Furthermore, they expect you to stop mooning over where you just came from, to put all that behind you so you can get with the program.

When you compare the adventures you have just completed to the pedestrian nature of your reentry life, depression seems a logical reaction. It *is* depressing to find that the same old problems you left behind are still there. People still argue about the same old disagreements. Whatever conflicts you put out of mind are still festering under the surface. The same responsibilities await you. The same constraints that held you back are still in place.

This process is called *reentry shock,* a term implying that some degree of upheaval is to be expected. Indeed, some people never really make the adjustment back home. After spending four years as a student at an American university, Miko returned to his native Japan. He was unprepared, however, for how restricted he now found his existence there. No longer could he tolerate the obedience, deference, and self-discipline that were expected by his family, employer, and culture. Within a matter of months Miko was back in the States: "I'm an American now in the way I think and act. My family didn't recognize me, nor did they like me very much. But this is now who I am."

It is so hard to come to terms with the implications of changes that occur during travel. Depression and disorientation are not uncommon during such transitions. Most of all, many of your relationships will never be the same again.

Impact on Your Friends and Family

The aftereffects of travel are certainly disruptive, at least if you were significantly affected by the experience. So much of the literature on the subjects of human growth and development speaks in the language of *individual* transformation, without consideration of the larger cultural context for behavior. This is especially the case in mainstream North America, where we emphasize ideals of freedom, independence, and autonomy far above other values such as cooperation, group responsibility, and interdependence that tend to be stressed in Asia, Latin America, and other parts of the world.

As is common in many books of this genre, I have been lauding the benefits of travel as a means to promote *self*-confidence, *self*-assurance, *self*-renewal, *self*-esteem, and *self*-determination. In other words, by its very nature as an activity that separates the individual from familial and cultural identity, the bias presented in our discussions has been that it is desirable to become more independent and self-sufficient, and that travel will help you do that.

It is important to consider, however, the consequences of such changes, especially when it comes time to return home. If one of the predictable results of travel is that it leads to greater independence, along with the confidence to carry through with your intentions, then this outcome is not necessarily good for the larger group of which you are a part. As we well know from research into the dynamics of families and groups, when any one individual in the system changes, then everyone else must change as well to accommodate themselves to the new elements. This is not a prospect that most people back home willingly embrace. You can, therefore, expect a lot of resistance to any new plans you intend to put into place.

When You Can't Leave Home to Travel

The principles presented in this book can be applied, with equal effectiveness, to any novel situation in which you face challenges. The key to personal change, whether at home or on the road, is to push yourself to take constructive risks, to get outside the boundaries of where you feel most comfortable, and then to redefine yourself in ways that are more desirable. It is certainly easier to do this when you're traveling, but once you've learned the process and applied it successfully, you can initiate other changes whenever you are sufficiently motivated.

The next best thing to traveling to the other side of the world is to entertain visitors in your own home. You can, in fact, be transformed as a result of interactions with a traveler. Whether you host an exchange student for a year, take on a boarder from another culture, or entertain guests for a weekend, you have the opportunity to learn about their worlds and hear about their unique views.

Think of all the ways you have been influenced, vicariously, through other people's experiences. Recall a particularly memorable book or movie in which you witnessed someone else's adventure and were changed as well. Over thirty thousand people sent letters to journalist Dominique Lapierre after reading his book *The City of Joy* (it was also a movie). Readers expressed their intense reactions to visiting, vicariously, the most crowded, poverty-stricken place in India. A television executive tells the author that the book widened her world and heart. One woman felt so inspired by the stories about Calcutta, she decided to adopt an Indian child. "Reading your book," she tells him, "so moved me that I had a feeling I *must* do something!"

Illusion and Imagination

We can indeed travel to other places by listening, watching, or reading other people's stories. Likewise we can travel with the illusion that we are leaving a part of ourselves behind just because we are away from usual influences and familiar settings.

Novelist David Adams Richards believes that although we may travel to escape something back home, this can never really happen as long as we bring ourselves on the trip; we carry with us exactly what we most wish to leave behind. "Therefore we can say with some measure of certainty that we never do go anywhere."

Travel is an illusion, a change of scenery that leaves the same protagonist on stage. Still, Richards explains, "If you aren't able to leave yourself behind when you travel you are at least able to take more of yourself with you, the farther you get from home."

What this means is that although you can't fully escape the past as you hurtle toward the future in a pressurized cabin at thirty-five thousand feet above the ground, you can leave parts of yourself behind, especially those behaviors, attitudes, and characteristics that most keep you from enjoying life more passionately.

Furthermore, you can be transformed by these experiences, as one man reveals: "When I was a kid, I saw *Lawrence of Arabia* on the big screen. I remember that one scene when Peter O'Toole is in the bar. He lights a match and then as he blows it out you are transported to this endless expanse of desert and blazing sun. I was utterly blown away. At that moment I thought to myself: 'I must go there. I must go everywhere!'"

It was at that moment that this man's hunger to see the world was born. He resolved, then and there, that travel would become an important part of his life. And it all started with a scene from a movie.

Just as powerful films and books can transform you through their vivid descriptions of people's experiences, so too can you be affected profoundly by your interactions with visitors in your own home. If, because of lack of funds or opportunity, you can't travel as often as you like, you can still build into your life transformative experiences through close interactions with others.

Under some circumstances, it is entirely possible to travel without leaving the comfort of your chair. Some people use their imagination to visit places all over the world and beyond; when they return from such mental excursions they may indeed be changed. This is one of the reasons that some people seek other dimensions by experimenting with hallucinogenic drugs to transport themselves to other worlds. In these and many other instances, travel takes place within the mind rather than the body.

A Spirit of Adventure

More than any other writer of this generation, Paul Theroux has chronicled the impact that travel has on the individual. Whether sailing through China, riding trains through Asia, or kayaking among a hundred islands in the South Pacific, Theroux has attempted to describe his inner journeys as much as the places he visited. His marriage in shreds, his health in decline, the final bleak news was the diagnosis of a suspiciously melanoma-like growth on his arm. Restless and despondent, he decided he couldn't wait for the biopsy results sitting still. In fact, he didn't much like living within his skin regardless of whether it was cancerous or not.

It was a journey he needed, and hopefully a transformative one at that. Equipped with a collapsible kayak, Theroux was determined to do something to heal himself: "My soul hurt, my heart was damaged, I was lonely . . . I wanted to be purified by water and wilderness."

He said good-bye to his wife, unable to imagine a life without her: "I tried to console myself by saying, *This is like going on a journey,* because a journey can be either your death or your transformation, though on this one I imagined that I would just keep living a half-life."

He was wrong, of course, and experienced traveler that he was, he should have known better. Theroux did heal himself on the road, or rather on the seas of the South Pacific. What began as a journey, "an experience in parentheses, enclosed by my life," turned into his life.

—⁓—

We think of travel as being separate from our normal lives, a respite, a moratorium, a time out that eventually ends once we return home. Yet each of us is traveling every moment of our lives, whether we define it as a vacation or not. Wherever you are, whomever you are with, whatever the circumstances, travel is a state of mind in which you attend to your movements through space, light, and time.

You need not be in Tahiti or Madagascar to be transformed by your journey. Taking a trip, even an adventurous, unstructured trip, is no guarantee that you will grow significantly and permanently as a result. Just getting out of bed in the morning in a particular way, facing the day with a spirit of adventure, encountering people with openness and flexibility, pushing yourself to do things differently, is what creates personal growth.

While it is often easier to do this on a trip, away from usual influences and restrictions, these changes can take place anywhere you choose to make them happen. In fact, if travel teaches you one important lesson it is that life is too sweet and short to limit your freedom to mere vacations. Travel is not really an escape from normal life, nor is it an insulated reality; rather, it acts as a reminder of what is possible for you to experience every waking moment of your life. Only then can travel change your life.

For Further Reading

Adler, J. (1993). Been there, done that. *Newsweek,* July 19, 42–48.

Alexander the Great. (1958). *The life of Alexander the Great.* Harmondsworth, England: Penguin Books.

Ambrose, S. E. (1996). *Undaunted courage.* New York: Simon & Schuster.

Atwood, M. (1994). The grunge look. In C. Rooke (Ed.), *Writing away.* Toronto: McClelland & Stewart.

Bangs, R. (1994). First date with misadventure. In R. Rapoport & M. Castanera (Eds.), *I should have stayed home: The worst trips of great writers.* Berkeley, CA: Book Passage Press.

Barnes, F. F. (1980). Travel and fatigue as causes of partial dissociative reactions. *Comprehensive Psychiatry, 21*(1), 55–61.

Benson, J. (1994). *Transformative adventures, vacations, and retreats.* Portland, Oregon: New Millennium.

Berendt, J. (1994). *Midnight in the garden of evil.* New York: Vintage Books.

Bombeck, E. (1991). *When you look like your passport photo, it's time to go home.* New York: HarperCollins.

Boorstein, D. (1983). *The discoverers.* New York: Random House.

Boud, D., Cohen, R., & Walker, D. (Eds.). (1993). *Using experience for learning.* Bristol, PA: Open University Press.

Brislin, R. W., Cushner, K., Cherrie, C., & Yong, M. (1986). *Intercultural interactions: A practical guide.* Thousand Oaks, CA: Sage.

Brookfield, S. (1993). Through the lens of learning: How the visceral experience of learning reframes teaching. In D. Boud, R. Cohen, & D. Walker (Eds.), *Using experience for learning.* Bristol, PA: Open University Press.

Bryson, B. (1993). *Neither here nor there: Travels in Europe.* New York: Avon.

Burke, K. (1995). Ten steps to paradise. *Outside,* January, 47–51.

Byrd, R. E. (1966). *Alone.* New York: Putnam.

Cade, B., & O'Hanlon, W. H. (1993). *A brief guide to brief therapy.* New York: Norton.

Campbell, J. (1968). *The hero with a thousand faces.* Princeton, NJ: Princeton University Press.

Cecil, J. (1992). *Traveling solo.* New York: HarperPerennial.

Crawford, M. S. (1993). Through Algeria. In M. Morris (Ed.), *Maiden voyages: Writings of women travelers.* New York: Vintage Books.

Crichton, M. (1988). *Travels.* New York: Knopf.

Csikszentmihalyi, M. (1990). *Flow: The psychology of optimal experience.* New York: HarperCollins.

Davidson, R. (1993). *Traveling light.* New York: HarperCollins.

Davies, R. (1994). Getting there. In C. Rooke (Ed.), *Writing away.* Toronto: McClelland & Stewart.

Dlugozima, H., Scott, J., & Sharp, D. (1996). *Six months off.* New York: Henry Holt.

Dumazedier, J. (1967). *Toward a society of leisure.* New York: Macmillan.

Eberhardt, I. (1993). The passionate nomad. In M. Morris (Ed.), *Maiden voyages: Writings of women travelers.* New York: Vintage Books.

Ewart, A. W. (1989). *Outdoor adventure pursuits: Foundations, models, and theories.* Columbus: Publishing Horizons.

Fraser, K. (Ed.). (1991). *Bad trips.* New York: Vintage Books.

Fulwiler, T. (1987). *Teaching with writing.* Portsmouth, NH: Cook Publishers.

Geertz, C. (1988). *Works and lives: The anthropologist as author.* Palo Alto, CA: Stanford University Press.

George, D. W. (1994). The flight from hell. In R. Rapoport & M. Castanera (Eds.), *I should have stayed home: The worst trips of great writers.* Berkeley, CA: Book Passage Press.

Gladding, S. T. (1996). Counseling and Mother Teresa: Lessons from Calcutta. *Counseling Today,* August, p. 28.

Goethe, J. W. (1968). *Italian journey.* New York: Schocken.

Gracen, D. (1994). Two bears dancing: A mid-life vision quest. *Women and Therapy, 15,* 147–159.

Hill, J. (1996). Meet Robert Young Pelton, *Outside,* May, p. 97.

Hoagland, E. (1991). Balancing act. In K. Fraser (Ed.), *Bad trips.* New York: Vintage Books.

Hopkins, R. L. (1994). *Narrative schooling.* New York: Teachers College Press.

Horn, R. (1995). No mountain too high for her. *Sports Illustrated,* April 29, pp. 2–4.

Huggan, I. (1994). Notes from the Philippines. In C. Rooke (Ed.), *Writing away.* Toronto: McClelland & Stewart.

Hymer, S. (1993). An alternative to the traumatizing vacation: The enriching, expansive vacation. *American Journal of Psychoanalysis, 58*(2), 143–157.

Iyer, P. (1994). Thousand and two nights. In R. Rapoport & M. Castanera (Eds.), *I should have stayed home: The worst trips of great writers.* Berkeley, CA: Book Passage Press.

Kiewa, J. (1994). Self-control: The key to adventure? *Women and Therapy, 15*(3), 29–41.

King, J. (1996). Kings of the road. *Calgary Herald,* August 10, p. G1.

Kinglake, A. W. (1845). *Eothen.* London: John Olivier.

Kottler, J. A. (1991). *The compleat therapist.* San Francisco: Jossey-Bass.

Kottler, J. A. (1994). *Beyond blame: A new way of resolving conflict in relationships.* San Francisco: Jossey-Bass

Kottler, J. A. (1995). *Growing a therapist.* San Francisco: Jossey-Bass.

Kottler, J. A. (1996). *The language of tears.* San Francisco: Jossey-Bass.

Krajick, K. (1992). Vision quest. *Newsweek,* June 15, pp. 62–63.

Krupp, J. A. (1995). Self-renewal, personal development, and change. *Adult Learning, 6*(3), 25–28.

Kurosawa, S. (1995). *The joy of travel.* Sydney: Angus & Robertson.

Lapierre, D. (1985). *The city of joy.* New York: Warner Books.

Laubscher, M. R. (1994). *Encounters with difference.* Westport, CT: Greenwood Press.

Leed, E. J. (1991). *The mind of the traveler.* New York: Basic Books.

Livermore, B. (1995). Safari with mom. *Women's Sports and Fitness,* September, pp. 46–79.

Mackey, M. (1994). Night of the army ants. In R. Rapoport & M. Castanera (Eds.), *I should have stayed home: The worst trips of great writers.* Berkeley, CA: Book Passage Press.

Manguel, A. (1991). The farther we are from England. In K. Fraser (Ed.), *Bad trips.* New York: Vintage Books.

Marchetti, C. (1994). Anthropological invariants in travel behavior. *Technological Forecasting and Social Change, 47,* 75–88.

Margoshes, P. (1993). The accidental travel writer. *Writer's Digest, 73*(8), 72.

Mayo, E. J., & Jarvis, L. P. (1981). *The psychology of leisure travel.* Boston: CBI Publishing.

Mitchell, R. G. (1983). *Mountain experience: The psychology and sociology of adventure.* Chicago: University of Chicago Press.

Morris, J. (1943). *Traveler from Tokyo.* London: Peters.

Morris, J. (1991). My worst journey. In K. Fraser (Ed.), *Bad trips.* New York: Vintage Books.

Morris, J. (1994). Bad things don't happen to me. In R. Rapoport & M. Castanera (Eds.), *I should have stayed home: The worst trips of great writers*. Berkeley, CA: Book Passage Press.

Morris, M. (Ed.). (1993). *Maiden voyages: Writings of women travelers*. New York: Vintage Books.

Morris, M. (1994). Introduction. In R. Rapoport & M. Castanera (Eds.), *I should have stayed home: The worst trips of great writers*. Berkeley, CA: Book Passage Press.

Nash, D. (1995). An exploration of tourism as superstructure. In R. Butler & D. Pearce (Eds.), *Changes in tourism*. New York: Routledge.

Packard, R. (1994). Which way is up? For some it's hard to tell. *New York Times*, October 16, p. 35.

Pearce, P. (1982). *The social psychology of tourist behavior*. New York: Pergamon Press.

Pitts, M. B. (1996). Reader survey results. *USA Weekend*, May 24–26, p. 4.

Plog, S. (1972). Why destination areas rise and fall in popularity. Paper presented at the Southern California Travel Research Association, October 10.

Raban, J. (1994). Road to utopia. *Australian Magazine*, October, pp. 15–16.

Richards, D. A. (1994). Travel. In C. Rooke (Ed.), *Writing away*. Toronto: McClelland & Stewart.

Roehl, W. S., & Fesenmaier, D. R. (1992). Risk perceptions and pleasure travel: An exploratory analysis. *Journal of Travel Research*, Spring, pp. 17–26.

Rose, A. (1995). The dynamics of personal growth, development, and change. *Adult Learning*, 6(3), 5–6.

Rubenstein, C. (1980). Vacations: Expectations, satisfactions, frustrations, fantasies. *Psychology Today*, May, pp. 62–76.

Schultheis, R. (1984). *Bone games*. New York: Random House.

Sharp, D. (1994). Time off for good adventure. *Women's Sports and Fitness*, Nov./Dec., pp. 56–89.

Sloan, G. (1996). Vacationers find their limits in Colorado. *USA Today*, August 30, p. 5D.

Spradley, J. P. (1980). *Participant observation*. Orlando: Harcourt Brace.

Stitsworth, M. H. (1989). Personality changes associated with a sojourn in Japan. *The Journal of Social Psychology*, 129(2), 213–224.

Thayer, H. (1993). *Polar dream*. New York: Delta.

Theroux, P. (1992). *The happy isles of Oceania*. New York: Ballantine.

Torrance, R. M. (1994). *The spiritual quest*. Berkeley, CA: University of California Press.

Tovey, P. (1993). *Smart vacations: The traveler's guide to learning adventures abroad.* New York: St. Martin's Press.

Tyler, A. (1985). *The accidental tourist.* New York: Knopf.

Ullman, J. R. (1947). *The age of mountaineering.* New York: Lippincott.

Wetzler, B. (1996). I hear America slogging. *Outside,* May, pp. 58–64.

White, R. W. (1995). Paradise fouled. *Outside,* June, pp. 37–41.

Willis, W. (1966). *Whom the sea has taken.* New York: Meredith Press.

Wilson, R. (1981). *Inside Outward Bound.* Charlotte, NC: East Woods Press.

About the Author

Jeffrey A. Kottler, Ph.D. is professor of counseling at the University of Nevada, Las Vegas, the base from which he begins his own transformative journeys to various parts of the world. He is the author of twenty-five books in the fields of psychology and education, including *On Being a Therapist, Growing a Therapist, Beyond Blame: A New Way of Resolving Conflicts in Relationships,* and *The Language of Tears.*

Index

Aboriginals, 18, 95–96, 153
Accidental Tourist, The (Tyler), 47–48
Accommodation phase, 130
Adam and Eve, 18
Adaptability, 58–60, 71–72
Adaption phase, 130
Addiction: to danger, 109; travel as, 23
Adjustment process, in cultural immersion, 129–131
Adler, J., 107
Adventure-based programs, 5, 74–75, 110–112
Adventure-based travel, 5, 18, 22–23, 103–113; motives for, 106–110, 151–152; and physical discomfort, 83, 104–105; and snobbery, 105–106; for something to prove, 106–108; unexpected, 112–113
African safari, 55–56
Airplanes, 49, 116
Alexander the Great, 18
Aloneness, 15; fear of, 15, 72
Altered state of consciousness: stress-induced, 108–110; travel as, 23–29, 76. *See also* Senses
Alternative lifestyle experimentation, 13; and acting out fantasies, 23–25
Alternative personas: and altered sense of self, 82–83; experimentation with, 13, 16–17, 67–68, 77; and imagining your future self, 142–143
Altruism, 100–102
Ambrose, S., 22
American Association of Retired Persons, 52
American Express, 134
Anthropological travel, 18, 94–100; and field notes, 155–156
Antianxiety medication, 66
Anxiety, 66
Appalachian Trail, 134–135

Arctic explorers, 73, 108
Armstrong, N., 7
Aruba, 11
Asia, 98–100
Assumptions, and perception of experience, 149–151
Attitude, 116–118, 127–129
Australia, 25, 51, 95–96

Backpacking, 24–25, 81
Bali, 94–95
Bangkok, 128
Bedford, S., 48
Beliefs, and perception of experience, 149–151
Benson, J., 53
Bodywork programs, 53
Bombeck, E., 48, 58, 131
Boorstein, D., 8
Boredom, 23–24, 79
Brief therapy, 132, 140–141; principles of, applied to brief travel, 141–147
Brief travel, 139–147; and brief therapy, 140–147; flexibility in, 146–147; focus on exceptions in, 145–146; focus on the present in, 143–145; goal definition for, 141–142; marathon action versus transformation in, 139–140; "miracle question" for, 142–143; principles of, 141–147; problem definition for, 141; "shock treatment" in, 147; small steps in, 146
Brislin, R., 121
Brookfield, S., 69
Buddha, 18, 101
Bungy jumping, 110
Burke, K., 136

Cain, M., 110
Campbell, J., 7
Camping, 24–25
Carpenter, W., 136

Casino resorts, 27–28
Cause-effect, altered sense of, 86–88
Cecil, J., 54
Change, travel as metaphor for, 8. *See also* Transformation
Chesterton, G. K., 87
City of Joy, The (Lapierre), 164
Clark, W., 7, 18, 22–23
Columbus, C., 3, 7, 154
Commercial travel, 18
Communication: and fear, 72; and losing your voice, 123
Companionship, 54, 55–58; versus solo travel, 54–55. *See also* Interaction; Relationships
Connectedness: and interaction with people, 90–94; sense of, 84–85. *See also* Interaction; Intimacy; Relationships
Conquest, 18
Control, letting go of, 44–49, 58–60, 63–64
Contructivism, 151–152
Convenience, 124
Cook, J., 3, 7, 18, 154
Costa Rica, 115
Council on International Education Exchange, 52
Crawford, M., 4
Critical incidents, 64–65, 121
Cruises, 57
Crusades, 2
Cultural differences: challenges of, 93–94, 121–122; and interaction with people, 91–102; openness to, 98–100, 122, 127–129, 131; in sense of cause-effect, 86–87; in sense of history, 80; in sense of time, 79; and social customs/ manners, 121–122; in tourism, 99
Cultural immersion: adjustment phases in, 129–131; and journal writing, 156–157, 158; stresses of, 126–131
Culture shock, 129–130

da Gama, V., 3
Danger: in adventure-based challenge, 108–110, 110; perception of, 110; of travel, 116–118. *See also* Glitches
Darwin, C., 18, 154, 155
Davies, R., 84
Depression, 145, 162
Desert Warfare School, 119
Destinations: choosing, 51–54; organized, 52–54
Developmental changes, 64–65
Dickens, C., 71

Differences, fear of, 72
Directions, asking for, 118–119
Discomfort, 83, 104–105; and appreciation, 123–124; and tribulations, 116–118
Discontinuous changes, 66–67
Disney World, 18, 27–28
Dlugozima, H., 135–136
Dorris, M., 114–115
Doubt, 73
Dumazedier, J., 24
Dupont, 134

Earhart, A., 107
Eberhardt, I., 4
Educational travel, 19–20; resources for, 52
Elderhostel, 52
Emotional arousal, and personal change, 69–70, 75
Emotional containment, travel for, 20–21
Emotional elaboration, travel for, 20–21
Empathy, 100
Entertainment, travel for, 27–28
Entry phase, 129
Equanimity, 131
Etiquette, 121–122
Exceptions, focus on, 145–146
Exchanges, 51–52, 163–164; resources for finding, 52. *See also* Homestays
Exile travel, 18
Expectations: and novelty as enabler of personal change, 62–63; and perception of experience, 149–151; and planning for the unexpected, 44–49, 58–60, 63–64; programmed, for personal change, 110; and unexpected adventures, 112–113
Experience: perception of, 148–154; reflective writing and, 154–160; vicarious, 164–165
Experimentation: in brief travel, 146–147; with new ways of being, 13, 16–17, 67–68, 77
Exploration, 18

Failure, fear of, 73
Family: as companions, 55–58; resistance of, to change, 12, 16–17, 160, 162–163; traveling on behalf of, 28–29. *See also* Relationships
Fantasies: acting out, 23–25; and traveling in imagination, 164–165
Fatigue, 129, 130
Fears, facing, 72–73, 75, 111
Field notes, 155–156. *See also* Journals

Fiji, 106
Flexibility, 58–60, 100, 146–147
Franz, C., 55
Freedom, perception of, 67, 75
Freud, S., 154
Friends: as companions, 55–58; resistance of, to change, 12, 16–17, 160, 162–163. *See also* Relationships
Fulwiler, T., 159

Geertz, C., 94–95
Gender differences, in emotional expressiveness, 20–21. *See also* Men; Women
Geology, and sense of history, 80
Glitches, 114–131; and appreciation, 123–124; attitude of embracing, 116–118; of being lost, 118–121; of cultural judgmentalism, 122; mental preparation for, 45–46; problem solving and, 125–131; of social etiquette, 121–122; and stressing out, 122–123
Goal setting, 141–142
Good deeds, 100–102
Grand Canyon, 123–124
Grand Tetons, 148
Greeks, 2
Greene, G., 117–118
Growing a Therapist (Kottler), 115
Guatemala, 86–87

Hackett, A. J., 110
Hahn, K., 5
Hallucinogenic drugs, 165
Hatha yoga programs, 53
Havasupai Reservation waterfalls, 123–124
Hawaii, 91–93, 98
Healing, travel for, 25–27, 165–166
Healing programs, alternative, 53
Hemingway, L., 21
Hero's journey, 7–9
Heroic travel, 18
Hillary, E., 18
Himalayas, 26
History, sense of, 79–80
Hoagland, E., 47
Holy Grail, 7, 9
Home: appreciation of, 87–88, 160–161; gaining a new perspective on, 87–88, 160–161; returning to, 131, 160–165; stresses of returning, 161–162; transformative travel while at, 163–165
Home exchanges, 51–52; resources for finding, 52

Homestays, 51–52, 163–164; impact of, on personal change, 62–63; resources for finding, 52
Hong Kong, 138
Hoover Dam, 138–139
Hopkins, R., 59
Huxley, A., 79

Imagination, 165
India, 26
Indiana, 26
Indispensability, illusion of, 137
Indulgence, travel for, 27–28
Insight-oriented therapy, 132
Insulation, 12
Intellectual curiosity, 19–20
Interaction: and asking for directions, 118–119; and asking questions, 97; as focus of travel, 89–102; and listening to stories, 97–98, 153–154; and personal connections, 90–94; and responsibility of travelers, 100–102; and stresses of cultural immersion, 126–129; and traveling like an anthropologist, 94–100. *See also* Relationships
Intimacy: and sense of connectedness, 84–85; and traveling with companions, 55–58. *See also* Relationships
Irritability phase, 129–130
Italy, 68–69, 87–88
Iyer, P., 105, 120

Japanese culture, 99
Japanese tour groups, 99, 139–140
Jarvis, L., 24
Jesus, 101
Journals, 13; content of, 157–160; finding meaning through, 154–160; sample entries in, 156–157; structuring, 155–157
Judgmentalism, cultural, 98–100, 122, 127–129

Kalaupapa, 98
Kottler, J., 20, 115
Krupp, J.-A., 66

Language of Tears, The (Kottler), 20, 115
Lapierre, D., 164
Las Vegas, 18, 27–28, 148
Latin America, 79, 129
Lawrence of Arabia, 18, 154
Lawrence of Arabia, 164–165
Leed, E., 6, 154–155

Leisure behavior, 24
Leisure class, 5–6
Leper colony, 98
Levi-Strauss, C., 105
Lewis, M., 7, 18, 22–23
Lewis and Clark, 7, 18, 22–23
Lindbergh, C., 18
Linnaeus, C., 18
Literary travel, 18
Livermore, B., 55–56
Lonely Planet Guides, 117
Long-term travel, 133–138; options for, 137–138; overcoming obstacles to, 135–139
Lost, being, 103–104, 118–121

Mackey, M., 115
Magellan, F., 7
Maiden voyages, 4
Maintenance of change, 13–14, 46; at home, 160–166; and reflective contemplation, 74–75. *See also* Reflective contemplation
Mamet, D., 86
Manguel, A., 65
Marchetti, C., 6
Marco Polo, 2–3, 7, 18
Matchmaker, The (Wilder), 107
Mattheissen, P., 26
Mature Outlook, 52
Maui, 91–93
Mayo, E., 24
Mead, M., 18, 154
Meaning: finding, at home, 160–165; finding, through journal writing, 154–160; and perception of experience, 148–154. *See also* Journals; Reflective contemplation
Meditation training programs, 53
Memories: creating indelible, 111; and constructing meaning, 152–153. *See also* Stories
Men: and adventure-based excursions, 5; and emotional dimension, 20–21
Mental preparation, 43–49
Middle Ages, 2–3
Migrant farm workers, 18
Miller, H., 47, 91
Mindset: for change, 12; for openness to cultural differences, 100
"Miracle question," 142–143
Mitchell, R., 151–152
Mohammed, 101
Molokai, 98
Monastery, 21

Money, and long-term travel, 134
Morris, J., 117
Morris, M., 4, 48
Moses, 7, 18
Motives for travel: of acting out fantasies, 23–25; of adventure, 22–23, 106–110, 151–152; clarifying personal, 14–16; emotional, 20–21; of healing, 25–27; hidden, 28–29; of indulgence, 27–28; intellectual, 19–20; and types of travel, 18–19
Mount Everest expeditions, 7–8, 107
Mountain climbing, 107, 108–110, 151–152
Mythology, 7–9

Napoleon, 18
Nash, D., 99
Nellis Air Force Base, 119
New Zealand, 116–117, 139–140
Nineteenth-century Western travelers, 3–4
No Limits, 110
Nomads, 2, 18
North America, cultural differences in, 79, 100
Northern California, 127
Novelty, as enabler of change, 62–63, 163

Objective setting: for brief transformative travel, 141; for transformative travel, 44
O'Hanlon, W., 142
On Being a Therapist (Kottler), 115
Openness: to cultural differences, 98–100, 122, 127–129; and flexibility, 58–60
Ordinary moments, 138–139
Organized programs, 52–54. *See also* Adventure-based programs
O'Toole, P., 164
Outdoor recreation, 24–25, 81, 107. *See also* Adventure-based travel
Outward Bound, 5, 74–75
Overlanders, 105

Packard, R., 118–119
Pain. *See* Discomfort; Physical challenge
Papua New Guinea, 131
Participant-observer, 94–97, 127
Past, focus on, versus present, 143–144
Peace, inner, travel for, 25–27
Peace Corps, 51, 58–59
People. *See* Family; Friends; Interaction; Relationships
Perkins, P., 105
Perry, R., 18

Peru, 156–157
Peter the Hermit, 2
Philippines, 84–85
Phoenicians, 2
Physical challenge, travel for, 22–23, 104–105; motives for, 105–110, 151–152; satisfaction of, 123–124. *See also* Adventure-based travel
Pilgrimage, 2, 18
Pittman, S. H., 8
Plains Indians, 18
Planning. *See* Preparation
Play, 85–86
Positive, focus on, 145–146
Preparation: and choosing a destination, 49–54; and choosing solo versus companionship travel, 54–58; for glitches, 121; mental, 43–49; for personal change, 61–76; for sabbaticals, 133–134, 136; for the unexpected, 44–49, 58–60, 63–64
Present, focus on, 143–145
Problem solving: challenges of, 125–131; and personal change, 70–71
Public commitment, 13

Questions: and asking for directions, 118–119; asking the right, 60; and being a snoop, 97; for planning, 44–46, 47

Raban, J., 54–55, 97
Rafting trips, 58
Reentry phase, 131, 161–162
Reentry shock, 162
Reflective contemplation, 13, 73–75, 76; through journal keeping, 154–160; and perception of experience, 148–154
Reflective phase, 130
Relationships: impact of individual change on, 162–163; impact of traveling together on, 55–58, 84–85. *See also* Family; Friends; Interaction
Resistance: of family and friends to accepting change, 12, 16–17, 160, 162–163; to taking sabbaticals, 135–138
Responsibility, 100–102
Retreats, 18, 53
Richards, D. A., 164
Rio de Janeiro, 152–153
Risk taking, 62; and emotional arousal, 69–70; and perception of freedom, 67; physical, motives for, 106–110; and safety, 68; and sharing with strangers, 154; and transformation at home, 163

Romans, 2
Roots, reconnection with, 80–81
Routine, 23–24; and resistance to taking sabbaticals, 137
Rwanda, 83

Sabbaticals, 133–138; options for, 137–138
Safe risks, 68
Salt Lake City, 142
Scenery, and heightened senses, 81
Schedule, transformative, 12–13, 45
Schultheis, R., 108–109
Scientific travel, 18
Scientific travel writing, 154–155
Scotland, 80–81
Scott, R., 18
Self: and group, 162–163; refashioning, 77–88; sense of, 82–83
Senses, heightened, 78–88; and adventure, 103–104; and cause-effect, 86–88; of connectedness, 84–85; of history, 80–81; and journal writing, 158, 159; of play, 85–86; of self, 82–83; of space, 81; of time, 79–80
Sharp, D., 133–134
Singapore, 125–126
Situational changes, 65, 75
Six Months Off (Dlugozima), 135–136
Snobbery, travel, 105–106. *See also* Judgmentalism
Solitary travel, 54–55
Solution-focused therapy, 142
South America, 129
Southeast Asia, 71–72
Space, altered sense of, 81
Spiritual travel, 18; in Middle Ages, 2
Spontaneity: planning for, 63–64; and the unexpected, 44–49, 58–60
Spradley, J., 95
Stevenson, R. L., 18, 118
Stitsworth, M., 62–63
Stories: creating, 115–116; learning from others', 97–98, 153–154; and reflection, 152–153
Stress, 122–123; and adjustment process, 129–131; of cultural immersion, 126–129; in returning home, 161–162. *See also* Discomfort; Glitches; Physical challenge
Styles of travel, in history, 3
Supernatural aid, 7
Swiss Germans, 79

Tabei, J., 107–108
Teachable moments, 68–69

Territorialism, 6–7

Thailand, 71–72

Thayer, H., 73, 108

Theme parks, 27–28

Therapy: brief, 140–147; listening to stories in, 154; long-term versus brief, 132, 143–144; and real world, 12, 16; and reflective contemplation, 73–74; and teachable moments, 68–69

Theroux, P., 118, 165–166

Third World travel, 26–27

Thoreau, H., 18

Time: altered sense of, 79–80, 129; and long-term versus brief travel, 132–133, 136–137. *See also* Brief travel; Long-term travel

Tourism: cultural differences in, 99; as motive for travel, 18; personal change possibility in, 105–106

Tourism industry: marketing techniques of, 24; size of, 5

Tovey, P., 52

Transformation: conditions conducive to, 67–76; developmental, 64–65; discontinuous, 66–67; enablers of, 61–64; impact of individual, on family/group systems, 162–163; motives for, 14–16; and motives for travel, 18–29; in ordinary moments, 138–139; in organized adventure programs, 110–112; in personal story example, 10–14; planning for positive, 67–76; predisposition and, 149–151; processes of, 12–14; of relationships, 55–58; sabotage of, by friends and family, 16–17, 162–163; situational, 65, 75; types of, 64–67. *See also* Maintenance of change; Transformative travel

Transformative travel: adventure in, 103–113; brief, 139–147; and characteristics of successful transformative travelers, 126–129; choosing a destination for, 51–54; conditions for change in, 67–76; creating meaning in, 148–166; glitches in, 114–131; heightened senses during, 78–88; at home, 163–166; long-term, 133–138; mental preparation for, 43–49; in ordinary moments, 138–139; organized, 52–54; people interactions in, 89–102; planning, 51–60; planning for personal change in, 61–76; planning for spontaneity in, 63–64; processes of change in, 61–64; questions for planning, 44–46, 47; refashioning the self in,

77–88; responsibility in, 100–102; solitary, 54–55; stages of, in lifetime, 50–51; time frames for, 132–147. *See also* Brief travel; Sabbaticals; Transformation; Travel

Transportation: and history of travel, 3; by type of traveler, 105

Travel: as altered state of consciousness, 23–29; categories of, 18–19; democratization of, 5–6; hierarchy of, 105–106; history of recreational, 1, 2–7; illusion of, 164; impact of, on relationships, 55–58; motivations for, 14–29; in mythology, 7–9; scientific, 18, 154–155; as universal metaphor of change, 8–9. *See also* Transformative travel

Travel snobbery, hierarchy of, 105–106

Twain, M., 18, 57, 117

Tweedie, E. B., 4

Tyler, A., 47–48

Ullman, J., 109–110

Unexpected: adventures, 112–113; planning for, 44–49, 58–60, 63–64. *See also* Glitches

University professors, 137

Unknown, fear of, 72

Urban II, Pope, 2

Utah, 101

Ventura, M., 27

Vicarious travel, 164–165

Vision quests, 53

Wales, Prince and Princess of, 3

Walter the Penniless, 2

Weight loss, 146

Wells, G., 23

Wetzler, B., 135

Wheeler, T., 117

Wilder, T., 107

Wilderness travel, 24–25, 81, 107. *See also* Adventure-based travel

Willis, W., 28–29

Wilson, R., 75

Women: and emotional dimension, 20–21; as explorers, 107–108; as nineteenth century travelers, 4

Writing, 13, 74, 154–160; and active learning, 159; scientific travel, 154–155. *See also* Journals

Xerox, 134